Quest

Second Edition

Intro

Listening and Speaking

Laurie Blass
Pamela Hartmann

McGraw-Hill

Quest Intro Listening and Speaking, 2nd Edition

Published by McGraw-Hill ESL/ELT, a business unit of The McGraw-Hill Companies, Inc. 1221 Avenue of the Americas, New York, NY 10020.

ISBN 13: 978-0-07-312828-3 (Student Book)
ISBN 10: 0-07-312828-7
1 2 3 4 5 6 7 8 9 VNH/PCC 12 11 10 09 08 07 06

ISBN 13: 978-0-07-326959-7 (Student Book with Audio Highlights)
ISBN 10: 0-07-326959-X
1 2 3 4 5 6 7 8 9 VNH/PCC 12 11 10 09 08 07 06

ISE ISBN 13: 978-0-07-111924-5 (International Student Edition)
ISE ISBN 10: 0-07-111924-8
1 2 3 4 5 6 7 8 9 VNH/PCC 12 11 10 09 08 07 06

Editorial director: Erik Gundersen
Series editor: Linda O'Roke
Production coordinator: James D. Gwyn
Cover designer: David Averbach, Anthology
Interior designer: Martini Graphic Services, Inc.
Artists: Jonathan Massie, Ron Mahoney
Photo researchers: David Averbach, Tobi Zausner

International Edition ISBN: 0-07-111924-8

 **McGraw-Hill**

www.esl-elt.mcgraw-hill.com

The McGraw·Hill Companies

●●●●● ACKNOWLEDGEMENTS

The publisher and authors would like to thank the following education professionals whose comments, reviews, and assistance were instrumental in the development of the Quest series.

- **Roberta Alexander,** San Diego Community College District

- **David Dahnke,** North Harris College (Houston, TX)

- **Mary Díaz,** Broward Community College (Davie, FL)

- **Judith García,** Miami-Dade College

- **Elizabeth Giles,** The School District of Hillsborough County, Florida

- **Patricia Heiser,** University of Washington, Seattle

- **Yoshiko Matsubayashi,** Kokusai Junior College, Tokyo

- **Ahmed Motala,** University of Sharjah, United Arab Emirates

- **Dee Parker and Andy Harris,** AUA, Bangkok

- **Alison Rice,** Hunter College, City University of New York

- **Alice Savage,** North Harris College (Houston, TX)

- **Katharine Sherak,** San Francisco State University

- **Leslie Eloise Somers,** Miami-Dade County Public Schools

- **Karen Stanley,** Central Piedmont Community College (Charlotte, NC)

- **Diane Urairat,** Mahidol Language Services, Bangkok

- **Pamela Vittorio,** The New School (New York, NY)

- **Anne Marie Walters,** California State University, Long Beach

- **Lynne Wilkins,** Mills College (Oakland, CA)

- **Sean Wray, Elizabeth Watson, and Mariko Yokota,** Waseda International University, Tokyo

Many, many thanks go to Marguerite Ann Snow, who provided the initial inspiration for the entire series. Heartfelt thanks also to Erik Gundersen and Linda O'Roke for their help in the development of the second edition. We'd also like to thank Dylan Bryan-Dolman, Susannah MacKay, Kristin Sherman, and Kristin Thalheimer, whose opinions were invaluable.

TABLE OF CONTENTS

Quest: The Series

Quest Second Edition prepares students for academic success. The series features two complementary strands—*Listening and Speaking* and *Reading and Writing*—each with four levels. The integrated *Quest* program provides robust scaffolding to support and accelerate each student's journey from exploring general interest topics to mastering academic content.

Quest parallels and accelerates the process native-speaking students go through when they prepare for success in a variety of academic subjects. By previewing typical college course material, *Quest* helps students get "up to speed" in terms of both academic content and language skills.

In addition, *Quest* prepares students for the daunting amount and level of listening, speaking, reading, and writing required for college success. The four *Listening and Speaking* books in the *Quest* series contain listening and speaking strategies and practice activities centered on authentic recordings from "person on the street" interviews, social conversations, radio programs, and university lectures. Listening passages increase in length and difficulty across the four levels.

The *Reading and Writing* books combine high-interest material from newspapers and magazines with traditional academic source materials such as textbooks. Like the *Listening and Speaking* books, the four *Reading and Writing* books increase in difficulty with each level.

Quest Second Edition Features

- New *Intro* level providing on-ramp to Books 1-3
- Redesigned, larger format with captivating photos
- Expanded focus on critical thinking and test-taking skills
- Expanded video program (VHS and DVD) with new lecture and updated social language footage
- Test-taking strategy boxes that highlight skills needed for success on the new TOEFL® iBT
- New unit-ending *Vocabulary Workshops* and end-of-book academic word lists
- Teacher's Editions with activity-by-activity procedural notes, expansion activities, and tests
- Addition of research paper to *Reading and Writing* titles
- EZ Test® CD-ROM-based test generator for all *Reading and Writing* titles

Quest Listening and Speaking

Quest Listening and Speaking includes three or four distinct units, each focusing on a different area of university study— anthropology, art, biology, business, ecology, economics, history, literature, psychology, or sociology. Each unit contains two chapters.

Chapter Structure

Each chapter of *Quest Intro Listening and Speaking* contains five parts that blend listening and speaking skills within the context of a particular academic area of study. Listening passages and skill-development activities build upon one another and increase in difficulty as students work through the five sections of each chapter.

Part 1: Introduction
- Thinking Ahead – discussion activities on photos introduce the chapter topic.
- Reading – a high-interest reading captures students' attention and motivates them to want to find out even more about the chapter topic.
- Discussion – speaking activities check students' understanding and allow for further discussion.

Part 2: Social Language
- Before Listening – prediction activities and vocabulary preparation prepare students for the listening. Strategy boxes provide students with practical strategies they can use immediately as they listen to conversations.
- Listening – a high-interest conversation (available in video or audio) between students on or around an urban university campus allows students to explore the chapter topic in more depth.
- After Listening – comprehension, discussion, and vocabulary activities not only check students' understanding of the conversation but also continue to prepare them for the academic listening activities in Parts 4 and 5.

Part 3: The Mechanics of Listening and Speaking
- Chapter-specific pronunciation, intonation, language function, and collocation boxes equip student to express their ideas.
- Content-driven language function boxes are followed by contextualized practice activities that prepare students for social and academic listening.

Part 4: Broadcast English
- Before Listening – prediction activities and vocabulary preparation prepare students for listening to a short passage from an authentic or simulated radio program.
- Listening – a high-interest authentic radio interview allows students to practice their listening skills and explore the chapter topic in more depth.
- After Listening – Comprehension, discussion, and vocabulary activities not only check students' understanding of the interview but also continue to prepare them for the academic listening in Part 5.

Part 5: Academic Listening
- Before Listening – prediction activities and vocabulary activities prepare students for listening to an authentic academic lecture.
- Listening – an academic lecture written by university professors allows students to practice their listening and note-taking skills. One lecture in each unit is delivered via video.
- After Listening – comprehension activities allow students to use their lecture notes to answer discussion questions.
- Put It All Together – a longer speaking activity provides students with the opportunity to connect all three listening passages and give a short presentation on the chapter topic.

Teacher's Editions

The *Quest Teacher's Editions* provide instructors with activity-by-activity teaching suggestions, cultural and background notes, Internet links to more information on the unit themes, expansion black-line master activities, chapter tests, and a complete answer key.

The *Quest Teacher's Editions* also provide test-taking boxes that highlight skills found in *Quest* that are needed for success on the new TOEFL® iBT test.

Video Program

For the *Quest Listening and Speaking* books, a newly expanded video program on DVD or VHS incorporates authentic classroom lectures with social language vignettes.

Lectures

The lecture portion of each video features college and university professors delivering high-interest mini-lectures on topics as diverse as animal communication, personal finance, and Greek art. The mini-lectures run from two minutes at the *Intro* level to six minutes by Book 3. As students listen to the lectures they complete structured outlines to model accurate note taking. Well-organized post-listening activities teach students how to use and refer to their notes in order to answer questions about the lecture and to review for a test.

Social Language

The social language portion of the videos gives students the chance to hear authentic conversations on topics relevant to the chapter topic and academic life. A series of scenes shot on or around an urban college campus features nine engaging students participating in a host of curricular and extracurricular activities. The social language portion of the video is designed to help English language students join study groups, interact with professors, and make friends.

Audio Program

Each reading selection on the audio CD or audiocassette program allows students to hear new vocabulary words, listen for intonation cues, and increase their reading speed. Each reading is recorded at an appropriate rate while remaining authentic.

Test Generator

For the *Quest Reading and Writing* books, an EZ Test® CD-ROM test generator allows teachers to create customized tests in a matter of minutes. EZ Test® is a flexible and easy-to-use desktop test generator. It allows teachers to create tests from unit-specific test banks or to write their own questions.

SCOPE AND SEQUENCE

Chapter	Listening Strategies	Speaking Strategies
UNIT 1 EDUCATION		

Chapter 1
Personality and Learning
 	
• Social Language:
  On the street interviews
• Broadcast English:
  Interview on stress and
  learning
• Academic English:
  Campus tour
	• Making Predictions
	• Guessing the Meaning from
	  Context
	• Previewing: Having Questions
	  in Mind
		• Giving Advice
		• Clarifying
		• Giving Suggestions
		• Brainstorming
		• Asking for and Giving
		  Permission

Chapter 2
Learning and Memory
 	
• Social Language:
  Conversation between friends
• Broadcast English:
  Interview on study skills
• Academic English:
  Presentation on learning styles
	• Listening for the Main Ideas
	• Listening for Examples
	• Guessing the Meaning From
	  Context
	• Making Connections
	• Using Graphic Organizers to
	  Take Notes
		• Agreeing and Disagreeing
		• Expanding the Conversation
		  by Giving Examples
		• Expressing Understanding
		• Taking a Survey
		• Asking How to Do Something
		• Using Ordering Words

UNIT 2 BUSINESS		

Chapter 3
Career Choices
 	
• Social Language:
  Conversation between students
  studying
• Broadcast English:
  Interview on student jobs
• Academic English:
  Presentation on a career center
	• Making Inferences from the
	  Sound of Someone's Voice
	• Guessing the Meaning from
	  Context
	• Listening for Specific
	  Information
	• Getting the Main Ideas from
	  the Introduction
		• Starting a Conversation
		• Offering and Accepting or
		  Refusing Food or Drinks
		• Asking for and Offering Advice

The Mechanics of Listening & Speaking	Critical Thinking Strategies
UNIT 1 EDUCATION	
• *Yes/No* Questions • *Like* and *Enjoy* • Reduced Forms of Words	• Making Predictions • Brainstorming • Asking for Clarification
• *Wh-* Questions • *It's good for* + Noun	• Noticing the Main Idea • Expanding the Conversation by Giving Examples
• *the* + Noun + *business* • Reduced Forms of Words • /θ/ vs. /s/	• Making Inferences from the Sound of Someone's Voice • Starting a Conversation

Chapter	Listening Strategies	Speaking Strategies
UNIT 2 BUSINESS		
Chapter 4 **Marketing for the Ages** • Social Language: Conversation about a new job • Broadcast English: Interview on market research • Academic English: Class lecture on personal finance	• Guessing the Main Idea • Listening for Reasons • Listening for the Topic • Knowing When to Take Notes	• Expressing an Opinion • Keeping a Conversation Going: Asking Questions • Keeping a Conversation Going: Responding
UNIT 3 SOCIOLOGY		
Chapter 5 **Connecting with Others** • Social Language: Conversation about how to meet people • Broadcast English: Interview on friends • Academic English: Presentation on campus clubs	• Listening for Opinions • Guessing the Meaning from Context • Organizing Your Notes	• Making Eye Contact • Giving an Opinion • Asking for an Opinion
Chapter 6 **Sports and Life** • Social Language: On the street interviews • Broadcast English: Interview on sports and mob behavior • Academic English: Presentation on college sports	• Guessing the Meaning from General Context • Listening for Causes and Effects • Listening for Solutions to Problems • Using an Outline to Take Notes	• Refusing to Do Something • Asking for Explanations or Examples • Giving and Getting Feedback

The Mechanics of Listening & Speaking	Critical Thinking Strategies
• Understanding Interjections • Noun Phrases • /I/ vs. /i/	• Using a T-chart • Knowing When to Take Notes
• Reduced Forms of Words with /t/ and /y/ • *It's easy/hard* + Infinitive	• Responding to Information on the Internet • Thinking Ahead
• *Play* and *Go* + Names of Sports • Reduced Forms of Words • /æ/ vs. /a/	• Guessing the Meaning From General Context • Discussing Information in New Situations • Using an Outline to Take Notes

Welcome

Quest Second Edition **prepares students for academic success.** The series features two complementary strands—*Reading and Writing* and *Listening and Speaking*—each with four levels. The integrated Quest program provides robust scaffolding to support and accelerate each student's journey from exploring general interest topics to mastering academic content.

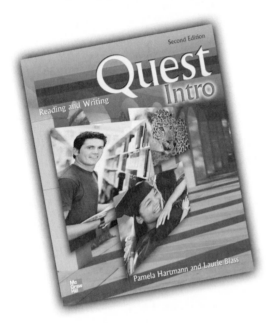

New second edition features

- New *Intro* level providing on-ramp to Books 1-3

- Redesigned, larger format with captivating photos

- Expanded focus on critical thinking skills

- Addition of research paper to *Reading and Writing* strand

- New unit-ending *Vocabulary Workshops* and end-of-book Academic Word List (AWL)

- Expanded video program (VHS/DVD) with new lecture and updated social language footage

- EZ Test® CD-ROM test generator for all *Reading and Writing* titles

- Test-Taking strategy boxes that highlight skills needed for success on the new TOEFL® iBT

- Teacher's Editions with activity-by-activity procedural notes, expansion activities, and tests

Captivating photos and graphics capture students' attention while introducing them to each academic topic.

UNIT 1

●●●●● EDUCATION

Chapter 1
Personality and Learning

Chapter 2
Learning and Memory

👥 **A. DISCUSSING THE INTERVIEW** Read the following sentences with a partner. Tell your partner if you agree or disagree.

1. Teenagers think differently from adults.

2. Eighteen- to 24-year-olds aren't very mature.

3. Students have trouble making decisions.

4. Students have trouble with time management.

5. Students have trouble memorizing things.

Speaking Strategy

Expanding the Conversation by Giving Examples

When you agree or disagree with someone, you will often give an example to explain your opinion. Some ways to give examples are *for example*, *for instance*, and *here's an example*.

Example: I disagree. Some 18-year-olds are very mature. Here's an example: My 18-year-old cousin gets good grades, takes care of his sick mother, and works part time.

👥 **B. EXPANDING THE CONVERSATION BY GIVING EXAMPLES** Read the sentences in Activity A again. Work with a new partner. This time give an example to explain why you agree or disagree.

PART ⑤ ACADEMIC ENGLISH An Introduction to Learning Styles

BEFORE LISTENING

Listening Strategy

Making Connections

You learned in Chapter 1 that it's good to connect the topic of a presentation, lecture, or interview to something that you already know. This will help you to focus and to understand more. To connect to the topic, try to think of at least three things that you already know about it.

Example: **Presentation Topic:** A Tour of City College
          Your Connections: Think about other colleges that you know.
                       Think about college websites that you visit.
                       Think about anything that you already know about City College.

👥 **A. THINKING AHEAD** You are going to hear a presentation about learning styles. Before you listen, make connections to the topic. In small groups, brainstorm everything that you remember about learning styles from Part 1 of this chapter (pages 26-28).

Listening and Speaking Strategies guide students to develop effective academic listening and note-taking skills.

Three high-interest listening selections in each chapter introduce students to the general education course content most frequently required by universities.

B. VOCABULARY PREPARATION Read the sentences below. The expressions in blue are from the conversation. Match them with the definitions in the box. Write the correct letters on the lines.

> a. become friends with people
> b. I don't know what will happen, but I'll probably have a good time.
> c. meet with and do something
> d. shared a lot of the same interests
> e. There are many people doing a lot of different things.

_a_ **1.** Sometimes it's hard to get to know people in a new place.

_____ **2.** Ashley and Viktor both liked biology, and they both liked golf. They had a lot in common.

_____ **3.** Mike might get together with someone in his study group.

_____ **4.** Rachel really likes big groups because there's a lot going on.

_____ **5.** Rachel said: "I don't know anyone at the party, but I'm going anyway. I'll take my chances."

LISTENING

A. LISTENING FOR MAIN IDEAS Listen to the conversation. As you listen, fill in the correct bubbles.

1. What event is happening tonight?

    Ⓐ a dance   Ⓑ a barbecue   Ⓒ a biology club meeting

2. Who is definitely going to the event?

    Ⓐ Ashley   Ⓑ Rachel   Ⓒ Mike

108   **UNIT 3** Sociology

PART 5 ACADEMIC ENGLISH
Thinking Critically about College Finances

BEFORE LISTENING

Credit cards

A. BRAINSTORMING You are going to hear a lecture in a business class. Before you listen, answer these questions with a partner.

1. What are some advantages of credit cards? What are some disadvantages of credit cards?

2. What advice can you give people about their first credit card?

3. Why are credit cards sometimes dangerous?

B. THINKING AHEAD What are some cultural **values**—ideas about what is important—in your culture? For each value in the chart, decide if your culture thinks it is good or bad (or possibly both good *and* bad). Check (3) your answers. Then, in small groups, compare your answers.

Values	Good	Bad	Both
Education			
Financial success			
Honesty (telling the truth)			
Laziness			
Giving to poor people			
Doing what is right, even when this is difficult			
Physical beauty			
Greed (wanting much more money than one needs)			
Hard work			
Working with other people			
Independence (not needing other people)			

92   **UNIT 2** Business

Gradual curve in each chapter from social language, to broadcast English, and then academic listening supports students as they engage in increasingly more difficult material.

Discussion, pair-work, and group-work activities scaffold the students' learning process as they move from general interest to academic content.

BEFORE LISTENING

Critical Thinking Strategy

Thinking Ahead

Often you know the topic of something that you are going to listen to before you listen to it. When you know the topic, think about it before you listen. Ask yourself questions about it. That way, you will be better prepared to listen.

A. THINKING AHEAD You are going to hear a radio interview with two people who **lost touch with** (stopped communicating with) each other. They wrote to each other for a long time and then stopped writing. Many years later, they found each other again.

Answer the questions in the chart below. Then write a question in the chart. Ask your partner the questions. Write your partner's answers in the chart. Compare answers.

Questions	My Answers	My Partner's Answers
If you lose touch with someone, what are some ways to find him or her again?		
Did you lose touch with someone? If yes, who? What happened?		
Your question:		

UNIT (2) VOCABULARY WORKSHOP

Review vocabulary that you learned in Chapters 3 and 4.

A. MATCHING Match the words on the left with the definitions on the right. Write the correct letters on the lines.

_g_	**1.** actually	**a.** ability
___	**2.** aptitude	**b.** bad point or characteristic
___	**3.** data	**c.** choose
___	**4.** disadvantage	**d.** give someone a job
___	**5.** greed	**e.** information
___	**6.** hire	**f.** shopping center
___	**7.** mall	**g.** really; in fact
___	**8.** pick	**h.** say "no"
___	**9.** refuse	**i.** things
___	**10.** stuff	**j.** wanting much more than you need

B. TRUE OR FALSE? Which sentences are true? Which sentences are false? Fill in T for *True* or F for *False*.

1. Cell phones and computers are examples of technology. Ⓣ Ⓕ
2. If you pay off a loan, you pay only the interest. Ⓣ Ⓕ
3. If you owe someone money, you need to pay them. Ⓣ Ⓕ
4. You cannot easily move something portable. Ⓣ Ⓕ
5. An internship can lead to a good job. Ⓣ Ⓕ
6. If you want to be careful with your money, it's a good idea to begin with a budget. Ⓣ Ⓕ
7. If you have to support yourself, you need to have a job. Ⓣ Ⓕ
8. You probably don't want to take a fabulous class. Ⓣ Ⓕ

Unit-ending *Vocabulary Workshops* reinforce key unit vocabulary that also appears on the High Frequency Word List.

COMPREHENSIVE ANCILLARY PROGRAM

Expanded video program for the *Listening and Speaking* titles now includes mini-lectures to build comprehension and note-taking skills, and updated social language scenes to develop conversation skills.

Audio program selections are indicated with this icon ⌒ and include recordings of all lectures, conversations, pronunciation and intonation activities, and reading selections.

Teacher's Edition provides activity-by-activity teaching suggestions, expansion activities, tests, and special TOEFL® iBT preparation notes

EZ Test® CD-ROM test generator for the *Reading and Writing* titles allows teachers to create customized tests in a matter of minutes.

UNIT 1

EDUCATION

Chapter 1
Personality and Learning

Chapter 2
Learning and Memory

Personality and Learning

Discuss these questions:
• Look at the picture. What are the people doing?
• How many hours a week do you study? How many do you relax?
• What classes do you enjoy the most? Why?
• Read the chapter title. What do you think the chapter will be about?

PART ① INTRODUCTION Know Yourself!

Mary is thinking about her future.

A. THINKING AHEAD A **major** is the main subject that a person studies in college*. A **career** is a person's lifetime **occupation** (job). Look at the picture. Then in small groups, answer these questions.

1. What occupations is the woman thinking about?

2. Match the majors and careers below. Write the correct letters on the lines. (Use a dictionary if necessary.)

Majors

_____b_____ **1.** biology

_____ **2.** chemistry

_____ **3.** education

_____ **4.** engineering

_____ **5.** medicine

_____ **6.** music

_____ **7.** theater arts

Careers

a. actor

~~**b.**~~ biologist

c. chemist

d. doctor

e. engineer

f. musician

g. teacher

*Americans usually use the word *college* to mean higher education in general. It can mean college or university.

B. READING: A WEBSITE www.planningforcollege.net is a website. It has useful information about college. In a section called "Ask Eric," people can ask all kinds of questions. Eric gives **advice** (suggestions). Read the website. As you read, think about this question: Does anything surprise you about Eric's advice?

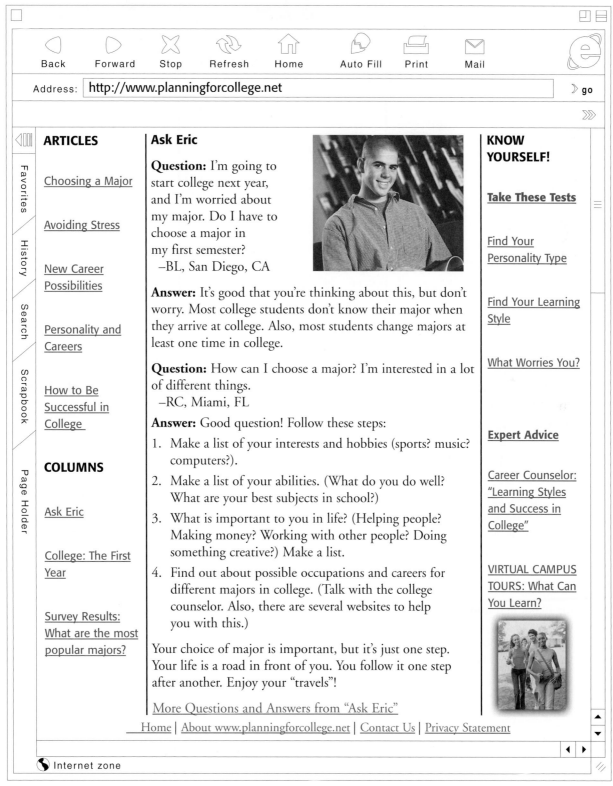

ARTICLES

Choosing a Major

Avoiding Stress

New Career Possibilities

Personality and Careers

How to Be Successful in College

COLUMNS

Ask Eric

College: The First Year

Survey Results: What are the most popular majors?

Ask Eric

Question: I'm going to start college next year, and I'm worried about my major. Do I have to choose a major in my first semester?
–BL, San Diego, CA

Answer: It's good that you're thinking about this, but don't worry. Most college students don't know their major when they arrive at college. Also, most students change majors at least one time in college.

Question: How can I choose a major? I'm interested in a lot of different things.
–RC, Miami, FL

Answer: Good question! Follow these steps:

1. Make a list of your interests and hobbies (sports? music? computers?).

2. Make a list of your abilities. (What do you do well? What are your best subjects in school?)

3. What is important to you in life? (Helping people? Making money? Working with other people? Doing something creative?) Make a list.

4. Find out about possible occupations and careers for different majors in college. (Talk with the college counselor. Also, there are several websites to help you with this.)

Your choice of major is important, but it's just one step. Your life is a road in front of you. You follow it one step after another. Enjoy your "travels"!

More Questions and Answers from "Ask Eric"

___Home | About www.planningforcollege.net | Contact Us | Privacy Statement

KNOW YOURSELF!

Take These Tests

Find Your Personality Type

Find Your Learning Style

What Worries You?

Expert Advice

Career Counselor: "Learning Styles and Success in College"

VIRTUAL CAMPUS TOURS: What Can You Learn?

C. APPLICATION Eric advises students to make a list of their interests, abilities, and the things that are important to them. Write your list in the chart below. (You may want to look back at Eric's advice for examples.)

My Interests	My Abilities	What Is Important to Me
Example: reading, nature, travel	English, Spanish, history	helping people, traveling, job security

D. TALKING ABOUT IT In small groups, share your chart. Which students have answers **similar to** (almost the same as) yours?

Example: **A:** Can I see your chart?
B: Sure, can I see yours?
A: Oh, look! We both like tennis.

E. JOURNAL WRITING Many students keep a journal. They use their journal to write their personal thoughts. Many students write in their journals every day. In this class, you will begin a journal. A good way to make a difficult decision or to explore your own ideas (and practice writing!) is to write in a journal. Grammar, spelling, and punctuation are not very important. Instead, *your thoughts* and *ideas* are important.

Choose *one* of the topics below. Write about it for five minutes. Don't worry about grammar. Don't use a dictionary.

• my major and how I chose it
• my idea of the perfect career
• my difficulty choosing a major
• something that worries me these days

BEFORE LISTENING

Which woman is probably calm?

Speaking Strategy

Brainstorming

Brainstorming is thinking of as many ideas as you can. When you brainstorm in a group, each person gives as many ideas as possible. You don't worry if the ideas are good or bad.

A. THINKING AHEAD In small groups, brainstorm answers to these questions: What causes people to have **stress** (worries about work, school, etc.) in everyday life? What causes students to have stress?

Critical Thinking Strategy

Making Predictions

Before listening to a radio program or lecture, it's good to think about what you will hear. Make **predictions** (guesses) about what people might say before you listen. When you make predictions, you will listen to find out if your predictions were correct or not. This will help you focus and understand more.

B. MAKING PREDICTIONS You are going to listen to people discuss what they do about stress. With a partner, make predictions about what the people will say. Which activities are **physical** (with the body)? Which activities are **mental** (with the mind)?

C. VOCABULARY PREPARATION Read the sentences below. The words in blue are from the interview. Match the definitions in the box with the words in blue. Write the correct letters on the lines.

> a. changes according to the situation
> b. happening again and again with the same time in between
> c. make less
> d. stress
> e. thinks deeply

_____a_____ **1. A:** What are your plans?
          B: It **depends**. I don't know. I may stay home. I may go to the beach.

_____ **2.** I have too much work right now. I need to find a way to **reduce** how many hours I work.

_____ **3.** Olivia has problems with money, work, school, and her boyfriend. All of these problems are causing her a lot of **anxiety**.

_____ **4.** Joel is a very calm person. I think it's because he sits quietly and **meditates** every morning.

_____ **5. A:** Do you play tennis **regularly**?
          B: Yes, we meet every Monday and Wednesday for a couple of games.

Listening Strategy

Guessing the Meaning from Context

When people speak, they often use words that will be new to you. Of course, you can't get out your dictionary to check the meaning of a new word in the middle of a conversation! You will need to guess the meaning from the **context**, the situation.

There are many ways to understand new words as you listen to someone speak. Here are two ways:

• Listen for the words *you know*. Sometimes you will hear an explanation after *you know*.
  Example: I like gardening–**you know**, planting flowers, watering, stuff like that.

• Watch the speaker's **body language** (movements with the hands and body).

LISTENING

A. LISTENING FOR THE MAIN IDEA Listen to the short interviews with eight people. As you listen, try to answer this question:

• Do most people do something *physical* or *mental* to reduce stress?

B. LISTENING FOR DETAILS Listen again. What does each person do? Write the information from the box in the chart.

deep breathing	gardening	meditation	tai chi
doesn't relax	hiking	running	~~yoga~~

Person	What does this person do?
1	*yoga*
2	
3	
4	
5	
6	
7	
8	

AFTER LISTENING

A. GUESSING THE MEANING FROM CONTEXT In the interviews, people explained the words and phrases in the box below with body language or after saying *you know*. Discuss the meaning of each with a partner. (You can use words or body language to explain.)

blow up	deep breaths	hiking	tai chi

B. TAKING A SURVEY Ask seven classmates this question: What do you do to reduce stress? Write their answers in the chart.

Example: **A:** What do you do to reduce stress?
                   B: I do yoga.
                   A: Yoga. (Writes *yoga* in the chart.) Thank you.

Classmate	What do you do to reduce stress?
1	
2	
3	
4	
5	
6	
7	

C. DISCUSSING SURVEY RESULTS In small groups, discuss the results of your survey. Answer these questions.

1. Do most of your classmates do something to reduce stress?

2. What were some activities that they talked about?

3. Which answers were different from answers in the interviews?

PART ③ THE MECHANICS OF LISTENING AND SPEAKING

INTONATION

🎧 Yes/No Questions

Yes/no questions are questions that have an answer of *yes* or *no*. When you ask a *yes/no* question, your voice goes up at the end.

Examples: May I ask you a question?

Are you planning to go to college?

🎧 **A. YES/NO QUESTIONS** Listen to each question. Repeat it after the speaker.

1. Are you a student here?

2. Do you know what your major will be?

3. Can I ask you something?

4. Do you enjoy hiking?

5. Are you stressed?

6. Do you like to work in the garden?

7. Are you majoring in business?

8. Do you have a job?

WORDS IN PHRASES

Like and *Enjoy*

Many words go together in **phrases**. It's important to learn these phrases, not just single words.

Like can be followed by a noun, a gerund (verb + *-ing*), or an infinitive (*to* + verb).

Examples:
I **like** music.	*Music* is a noun.
I **like listening** to music.	*Listening* is a gerund (verb + *-ing*).
I **like to listen** to music.	*To listen* is an infinitive (*to* + verb).

Enjoy can be followed by a noun or a gerund. *Enjoy* can **not** be followed by an infinitive.

Examples:
I **enjoy** movies.	*Movies* is a noun.
I **enjoy going** to the movies.	*Going* is a gerund.

When you use the negative, add *don't* or *doesn't*.

Examples:
I **don't like** pop music.
Adam **doesn't enjoy reading** books.

👥 **B. WORDS IN PHRASES** Go back to your list of interests on page 6. Tell a partner about these interests. Use the verbs *like* and *enjoy* in complete sentences. Then tell your partner four things that you *don't* like or enjoy.

PRONUNCIATION

◯ Reduced Forms of Words

Listening is sometimes difficult because when people speak quickly, some words become reduced, or shortened. For example, the word *because* may be reduced to *cuz*.

Also, when people speak quickly, two or three words are often pushed together. This can make them sound like one word. For example, *I don't know* becomes *I dunno*.

Examples:	Long Form		Reduced Form
	Because	→	**Cuz**
	Excuse me.	→	**'Scuse** me.
	I don't know.	→	**I dunno.**
	What's your name?	→	**Whatcher** name?
	What do you do?	→	**Whadaya** do?
	How do you spell that?	→	**Howdaya** spell that?
	Could you repeat that?	→	**Cudja** repeat that?

◯ **C. REDUCED FORMS OF WORDS** Listen to the conversations. You'll hear the short forms. Write the *long* forms on the lines.

1. **A:** What's your _____ name?

   B: Sarah.

   A: _____ spell that?

   B: S-A-R-A-H.

   A: _____ repeat that?

2. **A:** _____. May I ask you something?

   B: I _____. It depends.

   A: _____ do about stress?

   B: I try to exercise every day.

Critical Thinking Strategy ◖◖◖◖

Asking for Clarification

When talking with people, you will often need to ask them to **clarify**—make clear—what they said. Here are some ways to ask for clarification.

Examples:		
	Excuse me?	**Sorry?**
	Could you repeat that?	**What was that again?**
	Sorry. I didn't understand that.	**How do you spell that?**
	What does that mean?	

D. ASKING FOR CLARIFICATION With a partner, decide how to ask for clarification in the situations below. (In some situations, there are several ways to ask.) Use sentences from the Critical Thinking Strategy box on page 12.

1. You didn't understand the person because she was speaking very quietly.

2. You didn't hear the person because you weren't listening carefully.

3. You heard the person but didn't understand one word.

4. You heard the person, but there is one word that you need to see in writing before you can understand it.

LANGUAGE FUNCTION

Asking For and Giving Permission

To ask for permission, begin a question with *May I . . ., Can I . . .,* or *Could I . . .?*

Examples: **May I** borrow your pencil?
Can I close the door?
Could I see your class notes?

Here are common **replies** (answers).

Examples:
Sure.	Uh, I don't know.	Sorry, no.
Yes.	Um, I'm not sure.	No.
Yeah. (= yes)	Uh, it depends.	Nope. (= no)

Note: Use *um* and *uh* when you are thinking of an answer.

E. ASKING FOR AND GIVING PERMISSION Work with a partner. Follow the directions in the boxes below. Take turns. Student A begins.

Example: **A:** May I ask you a question?
B: Sure.

Student A

Ask Student B for permission to do the following things:
1. ask you a question
2. borrow a pencil
3. open the window
4. use your eraser
5. see your class notes

Next, answer Student B's questions.

Student B

Answer Student A's questions.

Next, ask Student A for permission to do the following things:
1. borrow your dictionary
2. close the door
3. sit here
4. tell you something
5. move this desk

PUT IT TOGETHER

FIND SOMEONE WHO Interview classmates about what they like or enjoy doing. Follow these steps.

When you ask questions:
1. Ask each person for permission to ask some questions.
2. Ask *yes/no* questions with intonation going up at the end. Use *like* and *enjoy* in your questions.
3. Find one person for each situation in the chart. Write that person's name on your chart only if he or she answers *yes*. Ask for clarification or spelling when necessary.

When you answer questions:
1. Give permission by using a reply that means *yes* or *maybe*.
2. When you hear the question, reply with an answer that means *yes* or *no* or *maybe*.
3. Be prepared to repeat, speak more clearly, or spell your name.

Example: **A:** May I ask you some questions?
B: Sure.
A: Do you like playing soccer?
B: No.
A: Do you enjoy watching old movies?
B: Yes.
A: Great. How do you spell your name?
B: A-L-E-X.

Find someone who likes/enjoys . . .	Name
playing soccer	
watching old movies	
astronomy (the study of the stars)	
exercising in a gym	
tennis	
animals	

PART ④ BROADCAST ENGLISH Stress and Learning

BEFORE LISTENING

A. THINKING AHEAD You are going to listen to a radio interview about stress and learning. What do you expect to hear? First, write your own answers to the questions in the chart. Then ask a partner the questions. Write your partner's answers.

Questions	My Answers	My Partner's Answers
Is stress always bad?		
How does stress **affect** (influence) the body?		
What can students do about stress?		

B. VOCABULARY PREPARATION Read the sentences below. The words and phrases in blue are from the radio interview. Match the definitions in the box with the words and phrases in blue. Write the correct letters on the lines.

a. answer	f. other thing(s)
b. become wet because you are hot	g. pushes other ideas out of my head
c. doing something about a difficult situation	h. strongly telling (someone to do something)
d. doing something later, not now	i. suggestion
e. organ of your body in your head; you think with it	j. things that happen because of
	k. understand

_____ **1.** I was really nervous. My hands began to shake and **sweat**.

_____ **2.** What are the physical **effects of** stress? What does stress do to the body?

_____ **3.** I asked Tom a question, but he didn't **respond**.

_____ **4.** My parents are **putting pressure on** me to study hard.

___e___ **5.** I can't think of the answer. My **brain** doesn't seem to be working!

_____ **6.** There is too much new information! I can't **take** it all **in**.

_____ **7.** We need milk, coffee, rice, and fruit. Is there **anything else**?

_____ **8.** How is Roger **coping with** his problem?

_____ **9.** I can't do it right now. I'm **putting it off** until tomorrow.

_____ **10.** I'm so worried about the exam! It's the only thing that I can think about. It **crowds everything else out**.

_____ **11.** Are you trying to choose a major? One good **tip** is to make a list of your interests and abilities.

LISTENING

A. LISTENING FOR MAIN IDEAS Listen to the radio interview. As you listen, try to answer these questions:
- Is stress always bad?
- Does the speaker give advice to students?

B. LISTENING FOR DETAILS Listen again. Check (✓) the answers that you hear. Each number may have more than one answer.

1. Stress makes _____.

_____ us relax   _____ us anxious   _____ our heart beat faster

_____ our hands shake   _____ our hands sweat

2. What advice does the speaker give students?

_____ Study harder.   _____ Study better.   _____ Ask questions.

_____ Be well organized.   _____ Use time wisely (well). _____ Learn to relax.

_____ Work with other students.

AFTER LISTENING

Speaking Strategy

Giving Advice

One way to give advice—suggestions—is with the words *should* or *shouldn't*.

Examples: You **shouldn't study** harder. You **should study** better.
              You **shouldn't** be afraid to ask questions. You **should ask** a lot of them.

A. DISCUSSING THE INTERVIEW The speaker said that students need to "study better." One way to study better is to ask questions. What else can you do to study better? In small groups, brainstorm ideas and make a list of good study tips.

Speaking Strategy

Clarifying

Sometimes when you ask a question or make a statement, the other person doesn't understand. When this happens, you need to clarify—explain—what you said. One way to do this is to say *I mean . . .* and then give an example or repeat the idea with new words.

Example: **A:** How can students be better students?
              B: Excuse me?
              A: **I mean,** what are some good study techniques? What can you suggest?

B. INTERVIEWING PEOPLE Interview three teachers at your school. Ask them for advice about how to study better. Follow these steps.

1. Ask for permission to ask each teacher two questions.
2. Ask their name (and how to spell it, if necessary).
3. Ask for their advice on how to study better.
4. If they don't understand, be prepared to clarify your question.
5. Write their answers in the chart on page 18.
6. Thank them for their time.

The next time your class meets, share the teachers' advice in small groups.

Teacher's Name	Advice on How to Study Better

PART ⑤ ACADEMIC ENGLISH
Finding Your Way: A Virtual Campus Tour

BEFORE LISTENING

Students taking a tour of a college.

 A. THINKING AHEAD You are going to listen to a person giving a virtual tour of the City College campus. Many students **tour** (visit and look at) different schools before they choose a college to attend. Sometimes they travel to visit the schools, but some schools also have **virtual** tours—tours on a computer.

Look at the map on page 19. What do you think the tour guide will say about City College? Brainstorm ideas with a partner.

B. VOCABULARY PREPARATION On the virtual campus tour, the tour guide uses some common prepositions of place.

1. Read the sentences below. Find the places on the map. In the sentences, prepositions of place are in blue.

The Learning Resources Center is **on your right**.
The Student Services Center is **on your left**.
The Student Services Center is **across from** the Learning Resources Center.
The snack bar is **next to** the Theater Arts Building.
The Student Services Center is **on the south side of** the campus.
The P.E. Building is **on the other (north) side of** the campus.
The tennis courts are **between** the P.E. (physical education) Building and the Campus Center.

2. With a partner, ask and answer questions about places on the map. Use prepositions of place.

Examples: **A:** Is the Student Services Center on the south side of the campus?
B: Yes, it is.

B: Is the Campus Center next to the Theater Arts Building?
A: No, it isn't.

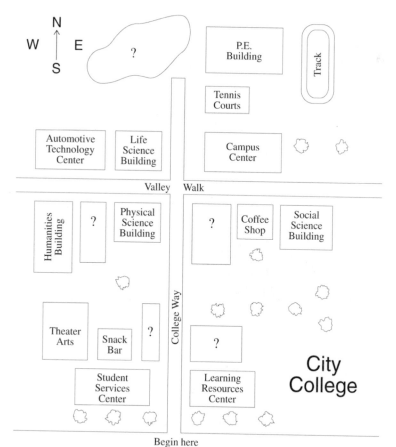

Listening Strategy

Previewing: Having Questions in Mind

It's a good idea to have a question or questions in mind when you listen to an interview, radio program, lecture, or presentation. Then when you are listening, you will listen for the answer(s). This will help you to focus and understand more.

A. LISTENING FOR MAIN IDEAS Look at the map and listen to the tour. As you listen, write the answers to this question on the map.

• What are the five places with question marks?

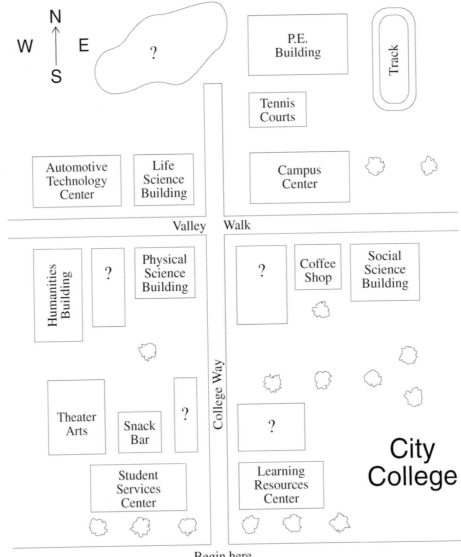

B. LISTENING FOR DETAILS Listen to part of the tour again. What classes can students take in these buildings? Check (✓) the classes that you hear.

1. What classes are in the Social Science Building?

   _____ psychology   _____ anthropology   _____ biology   _____ sociology

2. What classes are in the Physical Science Building?

   _____ chemistry   _____ ecology   _____ geology   _____ engineering

3. What classes are in the Humanities Building?

   _____ languages   _____ history   _____ film   _____ political science

4. What classes are in the Life Science Building?

   _____ biology   _____ astronomy   _____ food science   _____ physics

C. LISTENING TO A PERSONAL STORY Listen to Cassie talk about one service in the Student Services Building—academic counseling. **Academic counselors** give students advice about their classes, majors, and careers.

Before listening, read the questions below. Then listen to Cassie's problem and the counselor's advice. Fill in the correct bubbles.

1. What was Cassie's problem?
   Ⓐ She was having trouble in her psychology class.
   Ⓑ She was under stress and confused about her major.
   Ⓒ She was having personal problems.

2. What didn't her parents want her to study?
   Ⓐ psychology
   Ⓑ physics
   Ⓒ music

3. What will Cassie probably be after graduation?
   Ⓐ a music therapist
   Ⓑ a psychologist
   Ⓒ a musician

AFTER LISTENING

Speaking Strategy

Giving Suggestions

To give someone a suggestion (advice), use *can, could,* or *might.*

Examples: You **could** go to the academic counselor.
You **can** try the Learning Resources Center.
The college's website **might** be helpful.

GIVING SUGGESTIONS Work with a partner. Follow the directions in the boxes below and use the map on page 20. Take turns. Student A begins.

Example: **A:** I need to talk with a chemistry professor.
B: You could go to the Physical Science Building. It's to the west of the Social Science Building. I need to get advice about possible careers.
A: You might . . .

Student A

Tell your partner that you need to do one of the following things. Listen to your partner's suggestions.
1. talk with a sociology professor
2. find out about the swim team
3. find a quiet place to study
4. buy tickets to a student film
5. talk with a sociology professor

Next, listen to your partner and give suggestions. Tell your partner which building to go to and where it is. Use *can, could,* or *might* and prepositions of place.

Student B

Listen to your partner and give suggestions. Tell your partner which building to go to and where it is. Use *can, could,* or *might* and prepositions of place.

Next, tell your partner that you need to do one of the following things. Listen to your partner's suggestions.
1. get advice about possible careers
2. get some lunch
3. find a place to practice the piano
4. find a book
5. get some exercise

PUT IT ALL TOGETHER

 A. DOING RESEARCH Go to the website for a college or university. You can go to the website of one of the schools below or to any school that you are interested in.

- Santa Barbara City College (USA)
- Cornell University (USA)
- University of Oregon (USA)
- University of North Texas (USA)
- University of Toronto (Canada)
- Oxford University (England)

B. EXPLORING THE WEBSITE Look over a map of the school that you chose in Activity A. Take a virtual tour (or photo tour) if there is one.

Answer the following questions. Write your answers in the second row of the chart below:

1. What are some possible majors? (Are there any interesting or unusual majors?)

2. What is special or different about this college or university? For example,
   • can students learn tai chi, aikido, and soccer?
   • are there museums (how many?) on campus?
   • is there a marine diving program, and what does this mean?
   • can students learn to ride a horse?
   • can students put two majors together (in interdepartmental or interdisciplinary programs)?

C. SHARING WHAT YOU LEARNED In groups of three, talk about what you learned. Listen to the other students and write their information in the chart.

Name of the College or University	Interesting or Unusual Majors	Something Special or Different
Humboldt State University	aquarium sciences freshwater fisheries	Classes in hula dancing, ecology of tsunamis, wine-tasting, and bird-watching

CHAPTER 2

Learning and Memory

Discuss these questions:
- Look at the picture. What are the men doing?
- Do you like studying with friends or alone? Explain your answer.
- What is the best way for you to remember new information?
- Read the chapter title. What do you think the chapter will be about?

PART ❶ INTRODUCTION What Kind of Learner Are You?

| 1 | 2 | 3 |

Three different ways to learn

A. THINKING AHEAD People learn new information in different ways. In small groups, look at the pictures and answer these questions.

1. What are the people doing? How do you think each person is learning?

2. Match the number of each picture with the correct type of learning. Write the letters on the lines.

   _____ Picture 1   **a.** by seeing

   _____ Picture 2   **b.** by listening

   _____ Picture 3   **c.** by doing something

3. How do you learn best—by seeing, by listening, or by doing?

4. Do you think that you can become a better learner? If yes, how? If no, why not?

B. READING: TAKING A QUIZ Take the quiz on learning. Then read the explanation below.

What Kind of Learner Are You?

Do you want to become a better learner? Anyone can! To do this, first find out your learning style. (Your **learning style** is how you learn.) Take the following quiz to help you find out more about your learning style.

Complete each sentence. Fill in the bubble of the best answer for you.

1. I learn best when I _____.
- Ⓐ see information
- Ⓑ hear information
- Ⓒ do something

2. I like _____.
- Ⓐ pictures
- Ⓑ listening to tapes and stories
- Ⓒ working with people

3. In my free time, I like to _____.
- Ⓐ read
- Ⓑ listen to music
- Ⓒ play sports

4. I enjoy _____.
- Ⓐ thinking
- Ⓑ talking
- Ⓒ doing things

5. To remember a number, I _____.
- Ⓐ write it many times
- Ⓑ say it many times
- Ⓒ draw a picture

6. In a class, I learn best when _____.
- Ⓐ I have a good textbook
- Ⓑ the teacher is interesting
- Ⓒ I am doing activities

7. To study for a test, I _____.
- Ⓐ read my notes
- Ⓑ talk to other students
- Ⓒ study in a group

8. I plan my week by _____.
- Ⓐ making a list
- Ⓑ talking about it with someone
- Ⓒ making a calendar

9. I often remember _____.
- Ⓐ faces but not names
- Ⓑ names but not faces
- Ⓒ events but not names or faces

10. When I drive in a new city, I _____.
- Ⓐ use a map
- Ⓑ ask for directions
- Ⓒ drive around and find things by myself

Count the number of *A*s, *B*s, and *C*s:
Total **A** choices: _____
Total **B** choices: _____
Total **C** choices: _____

Explanation: If your choice was *A* most of the time, you generally like to learn by seeing. If your choice was *B* most of the time, you generally like to learn by listening. If your choice was *C* most of the time, you generally like to learn by doing. Which kind of learner are you?

Source: "Learning Style Inventory," *Peak Performance: Success in College and Beyond* (Ferrett)

C. TALKING ABOUT IT In small groups, share your answers to the quiz on page 27. How many students like to learn by seeing? How many like to learn by listening? How many like to learn by doing?

D. JOURNAL WRITING Choose *one* of these topics. Write about it for five minutes. Don't worry about grammar. Don't use a dictionary.

• my learning style
• my favorite subject in school
• something new that I learned recently
• the best way to memorize (learn and not forget) something

PART ② SOCIAL LANGUAGE Memory Tricks

BEFORE LISTENING

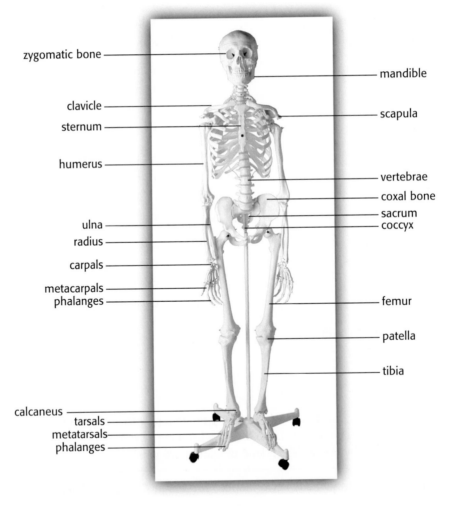

zygomatic bone
mandible
clavicle
scapula
sternum
humerus
vertebrae
coxal bone
sacrum
coccyx
ulna
radius
carpals
metacarpals
phalanges
femur
patella
tibia
calcaneus
tarsals
metatarsals
phalanges

Human bones

A. THINKING AHEAD Look at the picture on page 28. Discuss these questions with a partner:
  • What are some **techniques** (skills) for remembering a long list of words like this?
  • Which techniques work best for you?

B. VOCABULARY PREPARATION Read the sentences below. The words in blue are from the conversation. Match the definitions in the box with the words in blue. Write the correct letters on the lines.

a. groups of words with the same sound, usually at the ends of the words	**d.** a pile; many
	e. place
b. an important test; it usually happens in the middle of a course	~~**f.**~~ see a mental picture of
	g. words and expressions
c. memory tricks for remembering something more easily	**h.** a word that is made from the first letter of many words

_____f_____ **1.** I **imagine** hitting the ball before I do it. That way, I can hit it farther.

_____ **2.** Rachel has a **stack** of 3 by 5 cards. She writes new vocabulary on them.

_____ **3.** Ashley knows some good **mnemonics**. Her favorite one helps her remember the number of days in some months: "Thirty days has September, April, June, and November."

_____ **4.** Some memory tricks are **rhymes** such as *September* and *November*.

_____ **5.** Another way to remember things is to use an **acronym**. Michelle uses *FAN BOYS* to remember the coordinating conjunctions: *for, and, nor, but, or, yet,* and *so.*

3 by 5 cards
(3 inches by 5 inches)

_____ **6.** Mike can't believe the semester is half over. He has to take a **midterm** every day this week.

_____ **7.** You must memorize a long list of **terms** for the test next week.

_____ **8.** A mental map is a picture in your mind of a **setting**.

LISTENING

🎧 **A. LISTENING FOR MAIN IDEAS** Listen to the conversation. As you listen, try to answer these questions:

- What is Rachel worried about?
- How does Ashley help?

What colors are in a rainbow?

Listening Strategy

Listening for Examples

Speakers often give examples to explain difficult words or ideas. When listening, pay close attention to examples. This will help you understand more.

Examples often follow expressions such as *here's one, like,* and *such as.*

Examples: Ashley knows some good mnemonics. **Here's one:** . . .

Mike remembers a lot of mnemonics **like** . . .

To remember numbers, Rachel likes to use mnemonics **such as** . . .

B. LISTENING FOR DETAILS
Listen again. Match the type of mnemonic with the correct example. Draw arrows (→).

Types of Mnemonic

rhymes

acronyms

method-of-place technique

Examples

a mental map of a place you know to remember body parts

I before E, except after C.

Roy G. Biv for the colors of the rainbow

AFTER LISTENING

Speaking Strategy

Taking a Survey

There are many surveys in this book. When you take a survey, you ask different people the same questions or you answer other people's questions.

When you are asking the questions in a survey:
• Listen carefully to the answers.
• Show interest. (Say: "Oh." "Really?" or "That's interesting.")
• Take notes.
• At the end, thank the person. (Say: "Thanks," "Thank you," or "Thanks a lot.")

When you are answering questions in a survey:
• Speak clearly.
• Clarify if the person doesn't understand you. (See Chapter 1, page 12.)

A. TAKING A SURVEY Ask three classmates the questions below. Write their answers in the boxes on page 32.

1. Do you think that you have a good memory? Why or why not?
2. Do you use any memory tricks? Which ones?
3. What do you use them for?
4. What's the most difficult thing to remember? (For example, names, numbers, new vocabulary?)

Example: A: May I ask you some questions?

B: Sure.

A: What's your name?

B: Alex.

A: (Writes *Alex* in the box.) Do you think you have a good memory?

B: No, I don't. I . . .

Name: _____

Answer 1: _____

Answer 2: _____

Answer 3: _____

Answer 4: _____

Name: _____

Answer 1: _____

Answer 2: _____

Answer 3: _____

Answer 4: _____

Name: _____

Answer 1: _____

Answer 2: _____

Answer 3: _____

Answer 4: _____

B. DISCUSSING SURVEY RESULTS Form new groups, if possible. Discuss the results of your survey. Answer these questions.

1. Do most people think that they have good memories?

2. What memory tricks do people use? How do they use them?

3. Are there people who don't use memory tricks? Why don't they?

PART ③ THE MECHANICS OF LISTENING AND SPEAKING

INTONATION

🎧 *Wh-* Questions

When you ask *yes/no* questions, your voice goes up at the end of the question. When you ask questions with *wh-* (*who, what, where, when, why,* and *how*), your voice goes down at the end of the question.

Examples:

 Why?

Why not?

Who is it?

What's up?

How did you do it?

How does it work?

When does it start?

Where did they go?

🎧 **A. WH- QUESTIONS** Listen to the questions. Does the speaker's voice go up or down at the end? Circle the arrow that matches the intonation.

1.

2.

3.

4.

5.

6.

7.

8.

WORDS IN PHRASES

It's good for + Noun

Often there are words that go together. Words in a group are a phrase. It's important to learn words in phrases.

One phrase is *It's good for* + noun. You can use this phrase to explain a learning strategy or a memory trick. You can use other adjectives (such as *perfect* or *great*) in the place of *good*.

Examples: Here's a rhyme. **It's good for the days of the week.**

It's perfect for the colors of the rainbow.

It's great for body parts.

B. WORDS IN PHRASES Turn back to page 32. Look at the survey on memory tricks. Tell a partner about these tricks. Use *It's good/perfect/great for* + noun phrase in complete sentences.

LANGUAGE FUNCTIONS

Asking How to Do Something

Here are some expressions to ask how to do something:

How do/did you do it?   How did you do that?
What did you do?   How does it work?

Examples: A: I've got a memory trick. It's good for remembering body parts.
B: How does it work?

A: I memorized a hundred body parts.
B: How did you do it?
A: I used 3 by 5 cards.

C. ASKING HOW TO DO SOMETHING Listen to the sentences. Fill in the bubble of the best question.

1. Ⓐ How do you do it?

   Ⓑ How did you do that?

   Ⓒ What did you do?

   Ⓓ How does it work?

2. Ⓐ How do you do it?

   Ⓑ How did you do that?

   Ⓒ What did you do?

   Ⓓ How does it work?

3. Ⓐ How do you do it?

   Ⓑ How did you do that?

   Ⓒ What did you do?

   Ⓓ How does it work?

4. Ⓐ How do you do it?

   Ⓑ How did you do that?

   Ⓒ What did you do?

   Ⓓ How does it work?

5. Ⓐ How do you do it?

　Ⓑ How did you do that?

　Ⓒ What did you do?

　Ⓓ How does it work?

6. Ⓐ How do you do it?

　Ⓑ How did you do that?

　Ⓒ What did you do?

　Ⓓ How does it work?

Using Ordering Words

Sometimes you explain how to do something that has steps (things that you do in a certain order). Introduce each step with an ordering word. Some ordering words are *first*, *then*, *next*, and *finally*.

Example:　**First,** you memorize a setting or place in detail, like the street you live on. **Then** you remember a certain order in which you visit each place on the map. **Finally,** put the things you want to remember in that same order.

Expressing Understanding

When you tell people that you understand their explanation, you are expressing understanding. Here are some ways to express understanding:

O.K.
Oh.
Oh, yeah.
(Oh,) I get it.
} Informal

(Oh,) I see.
I understand.
I know what you're talking about.
} Formal

Example:　**A:** How did you do it?
　　　　　　B: First, I bought some 3 by 5 cards. Then I wrote each word on a card.
　　　　　　A: **Oh, I get it.**

　When might you use the informal expressions? When might you use the formal ones?

D. USING ORDERING WORDS AND EXPRESSING UNDERSTANDING Tell your partner how to do a memory trick. It can be one from this chapter or a new one. Use order words to describe each step. Then listen to your partner explain a memory trick and express your understanding.

PUT IT TOGETHER

EXPLAINING HOW TO DO SOMETHING Student A tells Student B how to do something that has many steps. Choose something that you know well. Here are some examples:

- how you get to school
- how to cook something
- how to drive a car
- how to make airline reservations online
- how to play a computer game

Use the correct intonation for *wh-* questions.
Use expressions for:

- asking for an explanation
- giving an explanation
- showing that you understand the explanation

Then Student B tells Student A how to do something that has many steps.

Example: **A:** I like to cook chili.

B: How do you do that?

A: First, I chop an onion. Then I cook the meat.

B: O.K. How do you do that?

A: In a pan on the stove.

B: I see.

A: Then I add a can of tomatoes and the onion to the meat.

B: O.K.

BEFORE LISTENING

A. THINKING AHEAD You are going to listen to a radio interview on **research findings** (information from experiments, interviews, or surveys) about the brains of young people (18 to 24 years old). Answer the questions in the chart below. Then ask a partner the questions. Write your partner's answers.

Questions	My Answers	My Partner's Answers
Do 18- to 24-year-olds act like older adults? Explain your answer.		
Do 18- to 24-year-olds think like older adults? Explain your answer.		
Is the brain of an 18- to 24-year-old different from other people's brains? How?		
What study and learning problems do some college students have?		

B. VOCABULARY PREPARATION Read the sentences below. The words and phrases in blue are from the radio interview. Match the definitions in the box with the words in blue. Write the correct letters on the lines.

a. aren't very good at	d. grow up	g. using time well
b. the basic parts of living things	e. look at again	h. very important
c. a counselor at school	f. problems	i. when we are talking about

_____a_____ **1.** Some college students **have trouble with** chemistry.

_____ **2.** I had a problem, so I went to see a **student advisor**.

_____ **3.** Biologists study **cells** to understand how they work.

_____ **4. Time management** is important for students.

_____ **5.** The ability to memorize is **crucial** for students.

_____ **6.** Stress is one of the **issues** that affect students.

_____ **7.** When you study for a test, **review** all the material.

_____ **8.** When is he going to **mature**? He still seems like a child.

_____ **9.** What does this mean **in terms of** how the brain works?

LISTENING

Critical Thinking Strategy

Noticing the Main Idea

The main idea of an interview, lecture, or presentation is the *big* idea. Sometimes, but not always, you will hear the main idea at the beginning of an interview, lecture, or presentation. Noticing the main idea will help you to organize the information you hear.

A. LISTENING FOR THE MAIN IDEA Listen to the interview. As you listen, try to answer this question:
- How are the brains of 18- to 24-year-olds different from the brains of older adults?

B. LISTENING FOR DETAILS Read the questions below. Then listen to the interview again. As you listen, fill in *T* for True or *F* for False. Listen again and check your answers.

1. Our brains are mature when we are teenagers. (T) **(F)**
   not

2. One part of the brain controls memories; it matures last. (T) (F)

3. Research shows that 18- to 24-year-olds may have trouble with decision-making. (T) (F)

4. Trouble with decision-making does not affect your ability to study and learn. (T) (F)

5. An example of active reading is making charts as you read. (T) (F)

6. It's a good idea to review new information within 24 hours. (T) (F)

Now listen again and correct the false statements. (See 1 above.)

Guessing the Meaning from Context

When people speak, they often use words that will be new to you. You will need to figure out the meaning from the **context**, the situation.

Here are two more ways to listen for the meanings of new words:

• Listen for a **synonym**, a word that means the same thing.

• Listen for an example. The speaker might say *for example* or *such as*.

C. GUESSING THE MEANING FROM CONTEXT Listen to a part of the interview. Listen for the meanings of these words. Fill in the correct bubbles.

1. **prune:**

   Ⓐ mature

   Ⓑ remove

   Ⓒ review

2. **read actively:**

   Ⓐ make a chart as you read

   Ⓑ review new information within 24 hours

   Ⓒ use time well

AFTER LISTENING

Agreeing and Disagreeing

Often when you speak with people you have to agree or disagree with what they say. Agreeing means that you think that what the person said is true. Disagreeing means that you think that what the person said is incorrect.

Agreeing:
I think that's right.
I agree.
That's right.
That's completely right.

Disagreeing:
I think that's wrong.
I don't agree. /I disagree.
That's wrong.
That's completely wrong.

A. DISCUSSING THE INTERVIEW Read the following sentences with a partner. Tell your partner if you agree or disagree.

1. Teenagers think differently from adults.

2. Eighteen- to 24-year-olds aren't very mature.

3. Students have trouble making decisions.

4. Students have trouble with time management.

5. Students have trouble memorizing things.

Speaking Strategy

Expanding the Conversation by Giving Examples

When you agree or disagree with someone, you will often give an example to explain your opinion. Some ways to give examples are *for example*, *for instance*, and *here's an example*.

Example: I disagree. Some 18-year-olds are very mature. **Here's an example:** My 18-year-old cousin gets good grades, takes care of his sick mother, and works part time.

B. EXPANDING THE CONVERSATION BY GIVING EXAMPLES Read the sentences in Activity A again. Work with a new partner. This time give an example to explain why you agree or disagree.

PART 5 ACADEMIC ENGLISH An Introduction to Learning Styles

BEFORE LISTENING

Listening Strategy

Making Connections

You learned in Chapter 1 that it's good to connect the topic of a presentation, lecture, or interview to something that you already know. This will help you to focus and to understand more. To connect to the topic, try to think of at least three things that you already know about it.

Example: **Presentation Topic**: A Tour of City College
Your Connections: Think about other colleges that you know.
Think about college websites that you visit.
Think about anything that you already know about City College.

A. THINKING AHEAD You are going to hear a presentation about learning styles. Before you listen, make connections to the topic. In small groups, brainstorm everything that you remember about learning styles from Part 1 of this chapter (pages 26-28).

B. VOCABULARY PREPARATION Read the sentences below. The words in blue are from the presentation. Match the definitions in the box with the words in blue. Write the correct letters on the lines.

a. learn	d. rewriting or restating	e. saying out loud
b. mostly	information and	f. give special attention
c. putting together	including only the	to the idea
	main ideas	

_____d_____ **1. Summarizing** is a good way to study for a test.

_____ **2.** When you study, **reciting** the main ideas is also a good idea.

_____ **3. Combining** two or three learning styles can help you learn better.

_____ **4.** Your learning style is **basically** the way that you learn best.

_____ **5.** I want to **point out** that you can always become a better learner.

_____ **6.** You can **figure out** the best ways to get to your classes by studying the campus map.

LISTENING

A. LISTENING FOR MAIN IDEAS Listen to Section 1 of the presentation. As you listen, write answers to these questions. After you listen, share your answers with a partner.

• What is a learning style? How many learning styles are there?

_____

_____

Now listen to Section 2 of the presentation. Try to answer this question:

• Why do you need to know your learning style?

_____

_____

Now listen to Section 3 and answer these questions:

• Can you combine learning styles? Why might this be a good idea?

_____

Using Graphic Organizers to Take Notes

When you listen to a presentation or lecture, take notes on the main ideas and the details. Taking notes while you listen helps you to focus. It also helps you to remember important information.

A graphic organizer can help you **visualize** (see in your mind) the main ideas and the details–the small ideas–in a presentation. It can also help you to visualize connections between ideas. An example of a graphic organizer is below.

 B. LISTENING FOR DETAILS Listen to the presentation again. As you listen, complete the graphic organizers to answer the questions.

1. What are the three types of learners? How do they learn?

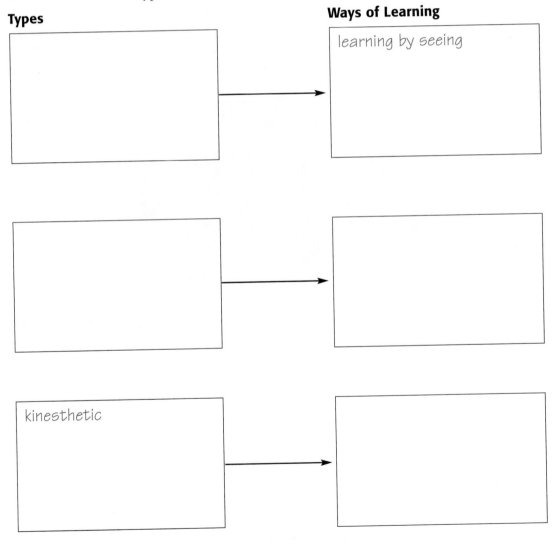

Types

Ways of Learning

learning by seeing

kinesthetic

2. What are some strategies for different learning styles?

Styles

Strategies

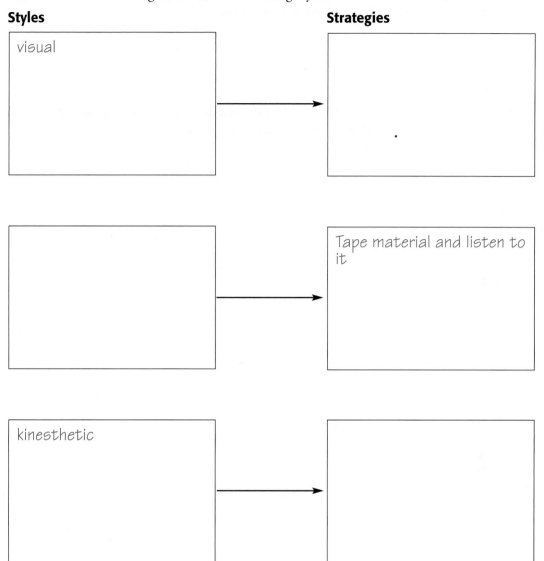

visual

Tape material and listen to it

kinesthetic

C. GUESSING THE MEANING FROM CONTEXT Listen to parts of the presentation. Listen for explanations of the words below. Write the meanings on the lines.

1. **dominant:** _____

2. **retain:** _____

MAKING CONNECTIONS In small groups, read about the four students below. They are studying for a biology midterm. They have lecture notes, textbook material, and word lists.

1. Dan likes to read, but he doesn't enjoy listening to lectures. His lecture notes aren't very good. He has a good memory.

2. Michael doesn't like to read, and he has trouble sitting quietly for a long time when someone is talking. He likes sports, and he enjoys drawing.

3. Emma doesn't like to read, but she likes to listen. She enjoys listening to music, lectures, and radio programs. She takes good lecture notes. She thinks that she doesn't have a very good memory.

4. Ashley has trouble with reading. She likes to get information from pictures. She has a very good memory.

Think about the presentation on learning styles. Look at your lecture notes. For each student, answer these questions:
• What kind of learner might he or she be?
• What strategies should he or she use?

PUT IT ALL TOGETHER

 A. DOING RESEARCH Go to the website for a college or university. You can go to one of the websites below or to the website of any school that you are interested in. Find information about the Learning Resources Center. (**Note:** Different colleges have different names for the Learning Resources Center.)
• North Carolina State University, USA (Counseling Center)
• University of Minnesota, USA (Supportive Services)
• Diablo Valley College, USA (Learning Center)
• University of Pittsburgh, USA (Academic Support)
• Western Washington University, USA (Academic Success)
• University of Auckland, New Zealand (Student Learning Centre)
• University of California, Berkeley, USA (Student Learning Center)

B. EXPLORING THE WEBSITE Go to the website for the school that you chose in Activity A. Answer the following questions about the Learning Resources Center. Write your answers in the first row of the chart below.

- Which college or university is it?
- What can you do there?
- What can you learn?
- Can you learn about your learning style?
- Can you learn to become a better student? How?
- Can you get a tutor (a person who helps you with a particular subject)?

C. SHARING WHAT YOU LEARNED In small groups, share your information. Tell the group what you learned. Listen to your classmates and write their information in the chart.

Name of the College or University	Things that You can Do at the Learning Resources Center

UNIT 1 VOCABULARY WORKSHOP

Review vocabulary that you learned in Chapters 1 and 2.

A. MATCHING Match the words on the left to the definitions on the right. Write the correct letters on the lines.

_b_ **1.** cells	**a.** answer
_____ **2.** effects	**b.** the basic parts of living things
_____ **3.** imagine	**c.** grow up
_____ **4.** mature	**d.** make less
_____ **5.** meditates	**e.** suggestion
_____ **6.** reciting	**f.** results
_____ **7.** reduce	**g.** saying out loud
_____ **8.** respond	**h.** see a mental picture
_____ **9.** terms	**i.** thinks deeply
_____ **10.** tip	**j.** words and expressions

B. TRUE OR FALSE? Which sentences are true? Which sentences are false? Fill in T for *True* or F for *False*.

1. A **visual** learner learns by doing.   (T) (**F**)

2. A **kinesthetic** learner learns by seeing.   (T) (F)

3. An **auditory** learner learns by hearing.   (T) (F)

4. "Roy G. Biv" is an **acronym**.   (T) (F)

5. A **rhyme** is a word that is made from the first letter of many words.   (T) (F)

6. When you **sweat**, you become wet because you are hot.   (T) (F)

7. If something is **crucial**, it isn't very important.   (T) (F)

8. **Mnemonics** can help you remember things.   (T) (F)

C. WHICH WORD DOESN'T BELONG? In each row, cross out the word without a connection to the other words.

1. student advisor	counselor	~~midterm~~
2. career	stress	occupation
3. crucial	auditory	visual
4. sweat	relax	meditate
5. imagine	recite	visualize
6. cells	test	midterm
7. stress	rhymes	anxiety
8. across from	opposite	virtual

D. HIGH FREQUENCY WORDS In the box below are some of the most common words in English. Fill in the blanks with words from the box. When you finish, check your answers in the reading on page 5.

best	~~interests~~	money	several	talk
different	life	people	something	well

1. Make a list of your _____*interests*_____ and hobbies (sports? music? computers?).

2. Make a list of your abilities. (What do you do _____? What are your _____ subjects in school?)

3. What is important to you in _____? (Helping people? Making _____? Working with other _____? Doing _____ creative?) Make a list.

4. Find out about occupations and careers for _____ majors in college. (_____ with the college counselor. Also, there are _____ websites to help you with this.)

BUSINESS

Chapter 3
Career Choices

Chapter 4
Marketing for the Ages

CHAPTER 3

Career Choices

Discuss these questions:
• Look at the picture. What is the woman doing?
• Do you think students should have part-time jobs?
• What kind of job do you want in the future? How will you get the job?
• Read the chapter title. What do you think the chapter will be about?

PART ① INTRODUCTION Should Students Work?

Working at the campus bookstore

Working at a computer company

Volunteering at a clinic

A. THINKING AHEAD Look at the pictures of students at work. In small groups, discuss these questions.

1. What is each person doing? Which one(s) might be earning money? Which one(s) might not be earning money?

2. What are some other jobs that students have?

3. What are some reasons for students to work?

4. Should students work? What are some **advantages of** (good things about) working while in school? What are some **disadvantages** (bad things)? Write your ideas in the chart on page 53.

Advantages	Disadvantages
job experience	no time for friends

B. READING: SHOULD STUDENTS WORK?

Read some emails between two college students. As you read, think about these questions: What are some reasons that students should work? What are some reasons that students should not work?

Subject: My New Job!
Date: Tuesday, May 17, 4:11 PM
From: Min <mpark@ccc.edu>
To: Daniel <dalvarez@ccc.edu>

Hi Daniel,

How do you like school this semester? I like my classes, but there's a lot of homework.

Guess what? I got a job! I work part time at the bookstore. I really need the money to help pay for school, and it's sort of fun and interesting.

What's new with you?

Min

Subject: Re: My New Job!
Date: Tuesday, May 17, 5:00 PM
From: Daniel <dalvarez@ccc.edu>
To: Min <mpark@ccc.edu>

Hey Min!

Good for you! I want a job, too, but my parents think that work will keep me from doing my homework. : (

Tell me more about your job.

(By the way, school is great. I like all my classes.)

Daniel

Subject: Working at the bookstore
Date: Tuesday, May 17, 5:11 PM
From: Min <mpark@ccc.edu>
To: Daniel <dalvarez@ccc.edu>

Hi Daniel,

I only work 12 hours a week. (They say that 15 hours are the most that students should work.) I'm learning a lot about the book business. I want to have my own business someday, so this is great experience.

Tell your parents that it's good for students to work! I read this at the college career center: "Studies show that students who work part time have higher **GPA**s (grade point averages) than students who don't work. In addition, 56 percent of college graduates in a recent survey said that they found their first job through work experience during college."

You're lucky that your parents are paying for school. You can get a **volunteer job** (work without being paid)! You could volunteer at a clinic. You want to be a doctor, so that way, you can get experience in your future career.

Min

Subject: Re: Working at the bookstore
Date: Wednesday, May 18, 7:00 PM
From: Daniel <dalvarez@ccc.edu>
To: Min <mpark@ccc.edu>

Hey Min,

Great idea! I forwarded your email to my parents. They said that it's O.K. to get a job, but I have to keep getting good grades. I'm going to follow your suggestion. I'm going to try to get a job at a hospital or a clinic.

Thanks!

Daniel

P.S. Let's get together soon!

C. TALKING ABOUT IT In small groups, discuss these questions:

- Do you have a job? If yes, what do you do? If no, would you like one? Why or why not?

D. JOURNAL WRITING Choose *one* of these topics. Write about it for five minutes. Don't worry about grammar. Don't use a dictionary.

- Should students work?
- my part-time job
- an **ideal** (perfect) part-time job for a college student

PART ② SOCIAL LANGUAGE
What Do You Want to Do with Your Life?

BEFORE LISTENING

A. THINKING AHEAD Read the careers in the chart. For each one, decide: Is it **cool** (fun or exciting)? Is it **practical** (realistic, useful)? Or is it both cool and practical? Check (✓) the correct columns in the chart.

Jobs	Is it cool?	Is it practical?	Is it both?
actor	✓		
biologist			
chemist			
doctor			
engineer			
movie director			
musician			
physical therapist			
psychologist			
teacher			

In small groups, share your charts. Then brainstorm at least 10 more jobs. Write them on the lines. Are they cool, practical, or both?

_____   _____

_____   _____

_____   _____

_____   _____

_____   _____

B. VOCABULARY PREPARATION Read the sentences below. The words and phrases in blue are from the conversation. Match the definitions in the box with the words in blue. Write the correct letters on the lines.

a. **get information about it**	e. **rest**
b. **made at home, not bought in a store**	f. **take as your main subject in school; specialize in; study the most**
c. **must give**	g. **very, very good; amazing**
d. **pay for your own expenses (rent, food, clothes)**	h. **why**

_____ **1.** I'm tired! Can we **take a break** now?

_____ **2.** Ashley makes **fabulous** cakes. Everyone loves them.

_____ **3.** No, I didn't buy the salad at the store. It's **homemade**.

_____ **4.** You have a good job. You can **support yourself** and pay for school.

_____ **5.** The career center has a list of campus jobs. I'm going to **check it out** and see if I can find a part time job.

_____ **6.** Emma, thanks for buying my business book. I think I **owe** you about $50, right?

_____ **7.** If you want to be an actor, you can **major in** drama at some universities.

_____ **8. A:** I went to academic counseling today.

        B: How come?

LISTENING

  • Why did Mike see a college counselor?
  • What is he trying to figure out?

B. LISTENING FOR DETAILS Listen again. Fill in the correct bubbles.

1. Where did Ashley get the cake?

    Ⓐ at the store

    Ⓑ Ashley made it.

    Ⓒ Someone made it.

2. What would Mike like to be after college?

    Ⓐ an actor

    Ⓑ a business person

    Ⓒ a rock musician

3. What suggestion does Ashley give Mike?

    Ⓐ He can study an instrument.

    Ⓑ He can study the music business.

    Ⓒ He can study business.

4. What is Mike's major?

    Ⓐ business

    Ⓑ music

    Ⓒ cooking

5. What do Ashley and Rachel say about Mike's career choice?

    Ⓐ It sounds cool.

    Ⓑ It sounds like it isn't practical.

    Ⓒ both A and B

Critical Thinking Strategy

Making Inferences from the Sound of Someone's Voice

Sometimes you can **make inferences about** (guess) a person's feelings. This helps you understand the person better.

To make inferences about people's feelings, listen to the sound of their voice, not just their words. The sound of a person's voice can tell you if the person is sad, happy, excited, worried, **embarrassed** (uncomfortable), angry, **certain** (sure), or uncertain. When you combine the words that you hear and the sound of a person's voice, you can often figure out his or her feelings.

C. MAKING INFERENCES FROM THE SOUND OF SOMEONE'S VOICE Listen to parts of the conversation. Make inferences about Mike's feelings. Fill in the correct bubbles.

Worried

Happy

Embarrassed

1. At first, Mike sounds _____.

   Ⓐ worried

   Ⓑ happy

   Ⓒ embarrassed

2. Next, Mike sounds _____.

   Ⓐ worried

   Ⓑ happy

   Ⓒ embarrassed

3. Then Mike sounds _____.

   Ⓐ worried

   Ⓑ happy

   Ⓒ embarrassed

AFTER LISTENING

A. TAKING A SURVEY Write your answers to the questions below in the chart. Then ask three classmates the questions. Write their answers in the chart.

1. What do you want to major in?

2. What career would you like to have?

3. Is the career **related to** (connected to) your major? If yes, how? If not, why not?

Example: **A:** Excuse me. May I ask you some questions?

B: Sure.

A: What do you want to major in?

B: Medicine.

My Answers	Classmate 1	Classmate 2	Classmate 3
1. _____	1. _____	1. _____	1. _____
2. _____	2. _____	2. _____	2. _____
3. _____	3. _____	3. _____	3. _____
_____	_____	_____	_____
_____	_____	_____	_____
_____	_____	_____	_____
_____	_____	_____	_____

B. DISCUSSING SURVEY RESULTS In small groups, discuss the results of your survey. Then discuss these questions.

1. Do most people know what they want to major in?

2. Do most people know what career they want to have?

3. Is there a connection between most people's ideas about majors and ideas about careers?

PART ③ THE MECHANICS OF LISTENING AND SPEAKING

LANGUAGE FUNCTION

"Some more coffee?"

Offering and Accepting or Refusing Food or Drinks

Here are some expressions for offering food or drinks:

Would you like some…?
Would you like some more…?
Some more…?

More…?
More?

Here are some expressions for accepting (saying yes to) or refusing (saying no to) food or drinks:

Accepting
Yes, thank you.
Yes, please.
Thanks.
That sounds good.
Sure.

Refusing
No, thank you.
No, thanks.
No more for me, thanks.

Examples:
A: **Would you like some** coffee?
B: **Yes, please.**
C: **No, thank you.**

A: **More** coffee?
B: **No more for me, thanks.**

A. OFFERING FOOD OR DRINKS Listen to and repeat the questions. Use the correct intonation.

1. Would you like some cake?

2. More cake?

3. Some more coffee?

4. Would you like some more coffee?

5. More?

B. ACCEPTING OR REFUSING FOOD OR DRINKS Student A offers Student B food or drinks from the box below. Student B accepts or refuses. Take turns. Use expressions from the Language Function box on page 60.

Example: **A:** Would you like some tea?
                B: No, thanks.

bread	ice cream	soda
cake	milk	soup
coffee	pizza	tea

WORDS IN PHRASES

> ## the + Noun + *business*
>
> You can combine many singular nouns with the word *business* to talk about careers.
>
> **Examples:**   the music business   the restaurant business
>   the movie business   the fashion (clothing) business
>   the banking business
>
> Notice that the first noun, the *kind* of business, is stressed.
>
> **Examples:**   the *art* business
>   the *computer* business
>   the *furniture* business

C. WORDS IN PHRASES With a partner, give advice to the people below. Take turns. Remember to stress the first noun in the phrase.

Example: **A:** Mike likes music and business.
                B: He should study the *music* business.

1. Emmy enjoys food and business.

2. Jason likes both movies and business.

3. Chris likes the Internet and business.

4. Max likes clothes and business.

5. Linda enjoys both paintings and business.

PRONUNCIATION

Reduced Forms of Words

When people speak quickly, two or three words often become reduced. They are pushed together so that they sound like one word. Here are some examples.

Examples:	Long Form		Reduced Form
	What am I **going to** do?	→	What am I **gonna** do?
	How about the music business?	→	**How 'bout** the music business?
	I'm **trying to** figure it out.	→	I'm **tryna** figure it out.

D. REDUCED FORMS OF WORDS Listen to these conversations. You are going to hear the reduced forms of some words. Write the *long* forms on the lines.

1. **A:** Hi, Emma. What's wrong?

   B: I lost my book. What am I _____ do?

2. **A:** Hey Emma, what's your major?

   B: I'm _____ figure that out.

3. **A:** I enjoy cooking and business. What should I study?

   B: _____ the restaurant business?

4. **A:** What's the answer to the first problem?

   B: I'm _____ figure it out.

5. **A:** I'd like to combine music and business.

   B: Well, _____ majoring in the music business?

LANGUAGE FUNCTION

 Asking for and Offering Advice

When you have a problem or need to make an important decision, you may want to ask someone for advice. Here are some expressions for asking for advice:

| So, what | do
can
should | I do? | | Well, what | do
can
should | I do? |

| What | do
can
should | I major in? |

When you think you can help someone with a problem or an important decision, you may want to offer him or her advice. You may want to put your advice into question form. Here are some expressions for offering advice in question form:

How about…?   Have you thought about…?   What about…?

E. ASKING FOR AND OFFERING ADVICE Work with a partner. Follow the directions in the boxes below. Take turns. Student A begins.

Examples: **A:** I love movies. What should I major in?
                      B: How about film history?

Student A

Tell your partner the following things about yourself. Ask for advice about your future. Use expressions from the Language Function box above.
1. enjoy seeing plays
2. enjoy sports
3. like clothes and business
4. like children
5. like the Internet

Now listen to your partner and offer advice. Suggest possible careers and college majors.

Student B

Listen to your partner and offer advice. Suggest possible careers and college majors. Use expressions from the Language Function box above.

Now tell your partner the following things about yourself. Ask for advice about your future.
1. like books
2. enjoy movies
3. enjoy cooking and business
4. like computer games
5. enjoy science

PRONUNCIATION

🎧 /θ/ vs. /s/

We use the letters *th* for different sounds. One of these is /θ/, the sound in *thank*. This sound is different from the /s/ sound. Listen to the sounds in these words. Can you hear the difference?

thank	→	sank		thick	→	sick
thing	→	sing		path	→	pass
think	→	sink		tenth	→	tense

F. REPEATING WORDS WITH /θ/ AND /S/ Now listen again and repeat the words in the box above.

🎧 **G. HEARING THE DIFFERENCE BETWEEN /θ/ AND /S/** Circle the words that you hear.

1. sing   thing

2. tenth   tense

3. sink   think

4. pass   path

5. sick   thick

6. thank   sank

👥 **H. PRONOUNCING /θ/ AND /S/** Student A says one of the words from the box. (Don't say the words in order.) Student B checks (✓) the word. Student A checks to see if the word is correct. Take turns.

some	thank	pass	tense
thumb	think	sick	path
thick	sink	tenth	sank

PUT IT TOGETHER

👥 **DISCUSSING WHAT YOU WANT TO DO WITH YOUR LIFE** In small groups, discuss what you want to do with your life. Talk about your idea of the perfect career, your difficulty choosing a major, or something that worries you.

Use expressions to ask for and offer help and the phrase *the* + noun + *business*. Remember to pronounce /θ/ and /s/ correctly.

Example: **A:** I don't know what to major in.

B: What do you like?

A: I like music, but it's not very practical. What should I do?

C: How about studying music and business?

A: Good idea.

D: Then you can work in the music business.

B: I don't know…

PART ④ BROADCAST ENGLISH Careers in Business

BEFORE LISTENING

Training a racehorse

Managing a coffee bar

Creating computer graphics

👥 **A. THINKING AHEAD** You are going to listen to a radio interview with three young adults. They are starting careers in business. The careers are **managing** (being the boss of) a coffee bar, **training** (preparing) racehorses, and creating computer graphics.

Make predictions on how young people might get jobs like these. Write your predictions in the chart. Then ask a partner about his or her predictions. Write them in the chart. Are your predictions similar or different?

Occupation	My Predictions	My Partner's Predictions
managing a coffee bar	Work part-time at a café during college	
training racehorses		
creating computer graphics		

B. VOCABULARY PREPARATION Read the sentences below. The words and phrases in blue are from the radio interview. Match the definitions in the box with the words and phrases in blue. Write the correct letters on the lines.

> a. an activity or event that leads to a goal
> b. choose
> c. a group of people who speak about something
> d. learn about
> e. a job that you learn about while you do it
> f. programs that tell a computer what to do
> g. services
> h. find

_____f_____ **1.** Ashley enjoys working with computers, and she learns new **software** programs very quickly.

_____ **2.** Don't let your parents **pick** your career. It's your life!

_____ **3.** Working in a restaurant is a **stepping stone** for Ashley. It will lead to a better job some day.

_____ **4.** The **panel** included three students. Each spoke about his or her job.

_____ **5.** How did you **come to** work on a farm?

_____ **6.** City College has the best career counseling **facilities** in the state.

_____ **7.** An **internship** is a great way to learn about a new career.

_____ **8.** Volunteering is another way to **explore** a new career.

LISTENING

Ben

Miriam

Luke

A. LISTENING FOR THE MAIN IDEA Listen to the radio interview. As you listen, try to answer this question:

• Is there only one way to explore a new career?

Listening Strategy

Guessing the Meaning from Context

In Chapter 1 you learned to listen for the meaning of new words by listening for a definition. Another way is to listen for an explanation. You can ask the speaker for an explanation. You might say *Can you explain that?* or *Can you tell me what that means?* The speaker then gives an explanation of the word or phrase.

Example:　　**A:** I got my job through an internship.
　　　　　　　B: Can you explain what that is?
　　　　　　　A: An internship is when you learn a job while you are doing it.

B. GUESSING THE MEANING FROM CONTEXT Listen to part of the program. Listen for and write the meanings of these words.

1. hot-walker: (Listen for a definition.) _____

_____

2. job-shadowing: (Listen for an explanation.) _____

_____

C. LISTENING FOR GENERAL INFORMATION Listen to the interview again. Match the person with the kind of work. Draw an arrow from the name to the kind of work.

Kind of Work: *horse training/hotwalker*

Type of Training: _____

_____

_____

_____

Ben

Kind of Work: *computer graphics* _____

Type of Training: _____

_____

_____

_____

Miriam

Kind of Work: *coffee bar* _____

Type of Training: _____

_____

_____

_____

Luke

Listening Strategy

Listening for Specific Information

Sometimes in class you have a set of questions to answer as you listen. These questions ask you to listen for **specific** (not general) information. When you have questions to answer, read the questions first. Make sure that you understand them. Then listen only for the answers to the questions.

D. LISTENING FOR SPECIFIC INFORMATION Listen again. Listen for specific information to answer the following questions:

- Which person has an internship?
- Which person did job-shadowing?
- Which person is in a management training program?

Write the answers in the boxes in Activity C on page 68.

AFTER LISTENING

Speaking Strategy

Starting a Conversation

Here are some ways to start a conversation in order to ask a question. It is polite to tell the person your **purpose** (reason) for starting the conversation:

Excuse me. May I ask you a question?
Excuse me. Do you have some time to answer a question?
Excuse me. I'm doing an assignment for my English class. May I ask you a question?

Example: **A:** Excuse me. May I ask you a question?
            B: Sure.

A. STARTING A CONVERSATION Ask three people who work at your school this question:

- How did you get your first job?
  Example: Excuse me. May I ask you a question? How did you get your first job?

Use the expressions from the box above. Write people's answers in the chart. Ask for clarification if you don't understand something.

Person 1	Person 2	Person 3

B. SHARING YOUR INFORMATION In small groups, share your chart. Did anyone do an internship? Was anyone in a training program? Did anyone do job-shadowing?

PART 5 ACADEMIC ENGLISH
An Introduction to the Career Center

BEFORE LISTENING

A. THINKING AHEAD You are going to hear a presentation about a campus Career Center. Before you listen, answer the questions in the chart. Then ask your partner the questions. Write your partner's answers in the chart.

Do you know how to . . .	My Answers		My Partner's Answers	
	Yes/No	If yes, how?	Yes/No	If yes, how?
get information on different careers?	Yes	Ask my business professor		
get information on different companies?				
write a **résumé** (a description of your skills and your work experience)?				
do well in a job **interview** (a meeting with an employer to talk about your skills and your work experience)?				
get a job?				

B. VOCABULARY PREPARATION Read the sentences below. The words and phrases in blue are from the presentation. Match the definitions in the box with the words and phrases in blue. Write the correct letters on the lines.

a. ability	g. important; useful
b. be certain	h. meet to get help from, for example, to find a job
c. gave a job to	~~i.~~ a person from an organization
d. give	j. prepare you for
e. giving advice or help	
f. helpful material, people, or activities	

_____i_____ **1.** A **representative** from Apple Computer is coming to campus this week. She's going to talk about job opportunities at the company.

_____ **2.** There are a lot of **resources** in the library: books, magazines, DVDs, CD-ROMs, and computers.

_____ **3.** Did you know that they **offer** free counseling at the Career Center?

_____ **4.** Ashley took an **aptitude** test. It helped her to figure out the best career for her.

_____ **5.** A major in business can **lead to** many different occupations.

_____ **6.** **Make sure** that you sign up for classes early. That way, you'll get the ones that you want.

_____ **7.** Apple Computer **hired** Jane right after she finished college.

_____ **8.** A part-time job can give you **valuable** experience. It can help you get a job later on.

_____ **9.** Many professors have **consulting** jobs with companies.

_____ **10.** Jane went to a class party because she wanted to **network with** the professor.

LISTENING

Listening Strategy

Getting the Main Ideas from the Introduction

You can get important information from the **introduction** (first part) of a presentation, lecture, or interview. In the introduction, speakers introduce the main topic and then say what the main ideas are. Listen for expressions such as *Today's presentation is in two parts; My presentation will **cover** (be about)…;* or *This presentation is on….*

Examples: **Today's presentation is in three parts.** I'm going to talk about auditory, visual, and kinesthetic styles.

My presentation will cover three learning styles: auditory, visual, and kinesthetic.

A. LISTENING FOR MAIN IDEAS Listen to the introduction to the presentation. As you listen, try to answer this question:
• What two topics will the speaker cover?

B. LISTENING FOR DETAILS Listen to Section 1 of the presentation. What services does the City College Career Center have? Check (✓) the ones that you hear.

_____ job listings: _____

_____ company tours: _____

_____ events: _____

_____ resources: _____

_____ tutoring: _____

_____ career counseling: _____

C. LISTENING FOR EXAMPLES Listen again. Listen for one example of each service that you checked above. Write the examples on the lines above.

D. LISTENING FOR DETAILS Listen to Section 2 of the presentation. How can you prepare for a career while you're a student? Write four things that you can do.

1. _____

2. _____

3. _____

4. _____

AFTER LISTENING

MAKING CONNECTIONS Read about the four students below.

1. Dan is a chemistry major. He also takes business classes. He enjoys cooking.

2. Michael doesn't know what to major in. He likes art, music, and children.

3. Emma is a computer science major, but she loves movies. She isn't sure what career is right for her.

4. Nicole is a business major. She loves books. She wants to have her own business someday.

Think about the presentation that you just heard. For each student, discuss these questions in small groups:

• What can he or she do to prepare for a career?
• What kinds of jobs (paid or volunteer), internships, and other things should he or she do?

PUT IT ALL TOGETHER

 A. DOING RESEARCH Go to the website for a college or university. You can go to the website of one of the schools below or to any school that you are interested in.
• University of British Columbia (Canada)
• Metropolitan College of New York (USA)
• Texas A&M International University (USA)
• Royal Melbourne Institute of Technology (Australia)
• Victoria University of Wellington (New Zealand)

 B. EXPLORING THE WEBSITE Go to the website of the school that you chose in Activity A. Do a search for "Career Center" or "Career Services." Answer the following questions. Write your answers in the first row of the chart on page 74.
• What services does the Career Center have?
• Does it have job listings? Events? Workshops?
• Can you learn how to write a résumé?
• Can you learn how to do well in an interview?
• Can you get career counseling?

C. SHARING WHAT YOU LEARNED Form groups of four. Each student in your group has information from a different website. Tell your group what you learned. Listen to your classmates and write their information in the chart.

Name of the College or University	Services at the Career Center
1.	
2.	
3.	
4.	

CHAPTER 4

Marketing for the Ages

Discuss these questions:
- Look at the picture. What is the man doing?
- What are your favorite stores? Why do you like them?
- Do you have a credit card? What are advantages and disadvantages of credit cards?
- Read the chapter title. What do you think the chapter will be about?

PART ❶ INTRODUCTION A Business Course Syllabus

The first day of class

Personal finance: dealing with your own money

👥 **A. THINKING AHEAD** Look at the pictures. Discuss these questions with a partner.

1. On the first day of class, what are some questions that students might have? (What do they want to know about the class?)

2. On the first day of class, most professors give their students a **course syllabus**—a paper with information about the class. What kind of information is probably on the syllabus? Try to think of seven things.

3. People need to learn to manage their **finances**—their money. What are some things that they need to know about? Try to think of five things.

B. READING: A COURSE SYLLABUS Read the course syllabus for a business class at City College. As you read, think about these questions: What do you understand about it? What don't you understand?

Business 154: Personal Finance
Course Syllabus

Dr. Chris Lee
MWF 10:00-10:50
Haines Hall 107
Office Hours: TTh 2:00-3:00

5 **Required Textbook**
Personal Finance (7th ed.) by Kapoon, Dlabay, and Hughes

Course Description
This is an introductory class in personal finance. You will learn to apply basic financial ideas to your own spending, saving, and investing habits. You will work on *critical thinking*—your ability
10 to use logic and solve problems. You will need to use critical thinking skills in this class and in most of your classes in college.

Course Requirements
You cannot be absent more than four times in the semester. There will be six quizzes on the material in the textbook. There will also be a midterm exam and a final exam. These exams will
15 cover material from both the textbook and the lectures in class. In addition, you must complete five critical-thinking exercises.

Grading
Your final grade in this class will be based on the following:

Quizzes	25%
Midterm Exam	20%
Final Exam	20%
Critical Thinking Exercises	20%
Class Participation	15%

20

Outline
25 Weeks 1–2   Personal financial planning
Weeks 3–4   Money management: the family budget
Weeks 5–6   Consumer education: how to be a smart shopper
Weeks 7–8   Credit and its use
Weeks 9–10   Market trends and the psychology of business
30 Weeks 11–12   Coping with taxes
Weeks 13–14   Investments (such as the stock market)
Week 15   Final exam week

C. VOCABULARY CHECK Look back at the syllabus. Find words and phrases that match the following definitions. Line numbers are given to help you find the words.

Definitions	Words and Phrases
ability to use logic and solve problems (Lines 9-10)	______________
small tests; not big exams (Lines 13-14)	______________
shopper (Line 27)	______________

D. COMPREHENSION CHECK In small groups, answer these questions about the course syllabus.

1. How many days a week does this class meet?
2. When can the students meet with the professor outside of class?
3. Who wrote the textbook?
4. Can students use information from this class in their own lives?
5. How many times can students be absent?
6. How much of a student's grade comes from the critical thinking exercises?
7. In which weeks will students learn about the psychology of business?

E. TAKING A SURVEY Some topics covered in the personal finance course are in the chart below. Follow these steps.

1. Read the topics. Look up any words that you don't know in a dictionary.
2. Think about your own answers to the questions.
3. Ask your classmates for their answers. Write their answers in the chart (𝍸 = 5 people said this, for example).
4. In small groups, discuss these questions: What do most students know about? What do most students want to learn about?

Topics	Do you know anything about this?		Do you want to learn about this?	
	Yes	No	Yes	No
Planning a personal budget				
Planning a family budget				
Being a smart shopper				
Using credit cards				
Paying taxes				
Investing in the stock market				

F. JOURNAL WRITING Choose *one* of these topics. Write about it for five minutes. Don't worry about grammar. Don't use a dictionary.

- my personal budget
- the advantages and disadvantages of credit cards

PART ② SOCIAL LANGUAGE Youth Trends

BEFORE LISTENING

👥 **A. THINKING AHEAD** A **trend** is something that is very popular—well-liked—for a while. It can be anything: a type of TV show, a hairstyle, a kind of **technology** (such as cell phones), or a type of music. Some trends don't last long. Other trends become part of society.

In small groups, discuss these questions.

1. Which age group is most interested in new trends? Why?
   - 8–24-year-olds
   - 24–38-year-olds
   - 38–50-year-olds

2. What's a popular TV show these days?

3. What's a popular clothing fashion?

4. Why are advertisers interested in trends?

B. VOCABULARY PREPARATION Read the sentences below. The words and phrases in blue are from the conversation. Match the definitions in the box with the words and phrases in blue. Write the correct letters on the lines.

a. agree to do; register	e. things
b. attracts; is interesting to	f. writer for a newspaper
c. short forms of words and phrases	g. young people
d. study to learn new information	

___g___ **1. Youth** are usually more interested in new trends than older people are.

_____ **2.** I need to be able to write very well because I want a career as a **newspaper reporter**.

_____ **3.** We have to **do research** in the library and online because we need to know something about credit cards.

_____ **4.** That music **appeals to** young people, but it doesn't attract older people. They aren't interested in it.

_____ **5.** People use many **abbreviations** when they are in Internet chat rooms; for example, FYI means "for your information," and ASAP means "as soon as possible."

_____ **6.** What kind of **stuff** do you email your friends about?

_____ **7.** That sounds like a great job! Where can I **sign up** for it?

LISTENING

Ashley and Mike learn about Rachel's new job.

A. LISTENING FOR THE MAIN IDEA Listen to the conversation. As you listen, try to answer this question:
• What is Rachel's new job?

B. LISTENING FOR DETAILS Rachel writes reports for a market research company. What does she report on? Listen to the conversation again and check (✓) the answers.

_____ youth trends

_____ what young people are wearing

_____ abbreviations in chat rooms

_____ popular TV shows

_____ what kinds of cell phones young people use

_____ what movies young people are seeing

_____ what books young people are reading

_____ what 24-to-38-year-old people are doing

AFTER LISTENING

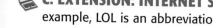 **A. TAKING A SURVEY** Follow these steps.

1. Write your own answers to the questions in the chart.
2. Ask two classmates the questions. Write their answers in the chart.

Questions	My Answers	Classmate 1	Classmate 2
What are some clothing trends these days?			
What are some new trends in movies?			
What kinds of cell phones are popular now?			
What are some abbreviations that you use in chat rooms or when you are instant messaging?			
What kinds of TV shows are popular now?			

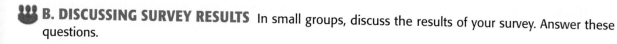 **B. DISCUSSING SURVEY RESULTS** In small groups, discuss the results of your survey. Answer these questions.

1. Did most students have the same answers? Explain your answer.
2. Do you agree with all the answers? Why or why not?
3. Did you learn about any new trends? If yes, which trends were new to you?

C. EXTENSION: INTERNET SEARCH What are some abbreviations that you can use in chat rooms? For example, LOL is an abbreviation for *laughing out loud*, or laughing a lot. Follow these steps.

• Check the most popular 25 abbreviations on this website (or find another):
  www.net-comber.com/acronyms.html
• Find at least five abbreviations that you like. Write them down.
• Share them with the class.

PART ③ THE MECHANICS OF LISTENING AND SPEAKING

PRONUNCIATION

🎧 /I/ vs. /i/

Some students have problems with the sounds /I/ and /i/. It might be difficult to hear the difference between these sounds, or it might be difficult to pronounce the difference. Listen to these words.

it	→	eat		his	→	he's
lid	→	lead		sit	→	seat
a pill	→	appeal		live	→	leave
bit	→	beet		itch	→	each
tin	→	teen		sick	→	seek

🎧 **A. REPEATING WORDS WITH /I/ AND /i/** Now listen again and repeat the words in the box above.

🎧 **B. HEARING THE DIFFERENCE BETWEEN /I/ AND /i/** Circle the words that you hear.

1. his	he's	**6.** live	leave
2. itch	each	**7.** sick	seek
3. sit	seat	**8.** a pill	appeal
4. lid	lead	**9.** bit	beet
5. it	eat	**10.** tin	teen

👥 **C. PRONOUNCING /I/ AND /i/** Work with a partner. Student A says one word in each pair. Student B circles the word. Then Student B says one word in each pair. Student A circles the word.

1. his	he's	**6.** live	leave
2. itch	each	**7.** sick	seek
3. sit	seat	**8.** a pill	appeal
4. lid	lead	**9.** bit	beet
5. it	eat	**10.** tin	teen

D. PRONOUNCING /ɪ/ AND /i/ IN SENTENCES Listen and repeat each sentence after the speaker.

1. I don't want to **eat it**.

2. May I **sit** in this **seat**?

3. **He's** changing **his** hairstyle.

4. They have to **leave** here and **live** in another place.

5. **A pill** will **appeal** to sick people.

INTONATION

Understanding Interjections

An interjection is a word, phrase, or sound. It expresses a short response in a conversation. Here are some common interjections in English. They are informal responses (answers). Notice their intonation.

Examples:	Interjections		Meanings
	Uh-huh.	→	Yes.
	Uh-huh!	→	Oh, *now* I understand.
	Hmm!	→	That's interesting.
	Huh?	→	What? Excuse me? (= I didn't understand or hear.)
	Uh-uh.	→	No.
	Uh . . . / Um . . .	→	I'm thinking. I don't know what to say.
	Uh-oh.	→	Problem!

E. UNDERSTANDING INTERJECTIONS Listen to the conversations. How does the second person respond? Check (✓) the correct meanings of the interjections.

Conversation	Yes.	No.	Oh, *now* I understand.	What?	I'm thinking.	Problem!
1		✓				
2						
3						
4						
5						

Work with a partner. Follow the directions in the boxes below. Take turns. Student A begins.

Example: **A:** Do you understand?
            B: Uh-huh.

Student A

Say each sentence to your partner. Wait for a response.
1. Do you have a job?
2. I can't find my book.
3. Exactly how many abbreviations do you know in English?
4. Are you wearing something black?

Now respond to your partner. Use the interjections in the box on page 83.

Student B

Respond to your partner. Use the interjections on page 83.

Now say each of these sentences. Wait for a response.
1. Are you wearing something white?
2. Do you like movies?
3. What's the most popular trend these days?
4. We have a big exam tomorrow.

WORDS IN PHRASES

Noun Phrases

Often when a noun comes before another noun, it is used as an adjective. In this chapter, there are many of these noun phrases. It's important to remember these two words *together*.

Example: The professor gave us a **course description** on the first day of class.
                                        adj.   noun

G. WORDS IN PHRASES Read the sentences. Find the noun phrases. Underline the nouns. Circle the nouns that are used as adjectives.

1. We're planning the (family) budget.

2. Ashley is taking a business course.

3. Rachel got a job as a trend spotter with that company.

4. She pays attention to youth trends everywhere.

5. A newspaper reporter needs to be a good interviewer and writer.

LANGUAGE FUNCTIONS

Keeping a Conversation Going: Asking Questions

A good conversation is like a **chain**: a question leads to an answer, and this answer leads to another question.

Asking questions is an important **technique** (way) to keep a conversation going. To ask questions, you need to understand the grammar of questions.

Yes/No Questions
Is that a good job?
Are you in the music business?
Do you **use** a computer?
Can you **travel** as part of your job?

Wh- Questions
Who **is** she?
Where **do** you **spend** most of your time?
Why **do** you **like** it?
How **can** a person **get** this kind of job?

Keeping a Conversation Going: Responding

People such as newspaper reporters are good at keeping a conversation going. They ask questions, listen to the answers, and respond. Often, they respond with another question, an interjection (*Oh, Hmm,* etc.), or new information. Many times they respond in more than one way.

Example:
A: What are some popular trends in technology? **(Question)**
B: I think devices like iPods are very popular. **(Answer)** I love my iPod. **(New information)**
A: Oh. **(Interjection)** What do you like about it? **(Question)**
B: I like how small it is and that I can listen to music on the bus. **(Answer)**
What do you do on the bus? **(Question)**

H. KEEPING A CONVERSATION GOING Read the conversations below with a partner. What is a good response for each one? Write a response on the line. (There are many possible responses.) Then practice the conversations.

1. **A:** Do you like your job?

   B: Yes, I like it a lot.

   A: _____

2. **A:** Do you work in an office?

   B: No, not now.

   A: _____

3. **A:** How much education do you need for this job?

   B: You need at least four years of college.

   A: _____

4. **A:** Do you use a computer in your work?

   B: Yes, it's really important.

   A: _____

5. **A:** What's one advantage of your job?

   B: Um, well, it's a good stepping-stone to other jobs.

   A: _____

6. **A:** What's a disadvantage?

   B: There's a lot of stress.

   A: _____

7. **A:** What was your major in college?

   B: I majored in marine biology.

   A: _____

8. **A:** What do you do?

   B: I'm a trend spotter.

   A: _____

PUT IT TOGETHER

INTERVIEWING SOMEONE In small groups, follow these steps.

1. One student chooses an occupation from the box.

actor	career counselor	hair stylist	pilot
animal trainer	chemist	mechanic	psychologist
banker	doctor	movie director	restaurant owner
biologist	fashion designer	musician	teacher

2. The other students ask a chain of questions to guess this occupation.

   • You can ask almost anything, but do not ask: What do you do? What career (or occupation) do you have? What kind of work do you do?

   • Use the questions in Activity H on pages 85-86, or you can use your own questions.

   • Listen carefully to each answer. Respond with an interjection and ask another question.

   • Try to guess which occupation the first student chose. Stop when someone guesses correctly.

3. Then another student chooses another occupation. Repeat Step 2.

   Example: (Student A chooses an occupation.)

   B: Do you use a computer at work?

   A: Yes, I use a computer every day.

   C: Hmm. Is your job cool?

   A: No.

PART ④ BROADCAST ENGLISH What's Hot, What's Not

BEFORE LISTENING

High school kids **hanging out** at a **mall**.

A. THINKING AHEAD You are going to listen to a radio interview with Tina Lane. Tina owns a market research company. With a partner, make predictions about her company. Discuss the questions below. (Don't worry about your answers being right.)

1. Why does Tina's company collect information from kids?

2. Where does Tina find the kids who give her information?

3. What does Tina's company do with the information?

4. What kind of technology are kids **into**? (What technology is very popular with kids?)

5. Kids buy things at a shopping mall, but what **else** (other things) do they do at a mall?

B. VOCABULARY PREPARATION Read the sentences below. The words in blue are from the radio interview. Match the words in blue with the definitions in the box. Write the correct letters on the lines.

a. in fact; the truth is that...	e. recognize
b. distribute; send to many people	f. a step-by-step way of doing something
c. a natural understanding of something	g. useful information
d. people who write advertisements (ads)	h. very, very popular

_____e_____ **1.** Most high school students can **spot** new trends very quickly. They see trends at school, at the mall, in movies, and on the Internet.

_____ **2.** Some people think that kids don't have much money to spend, but **actually**, they do, and they *begin* most trends.

_____ **3.** This style is very **hot** right now. Everyone wants it.

_____ **4.** Ordinary conversations between young people about clothes and movies are **valuable data** to trend spotters.

_____ **5.** The **advertisers** for that car are spending a lot of money to sell it on TV.

_____ **6.** Some business people have good **intuition** about what will be popular in the future. They can't explain how they know what will be popular, but they are right.

_____ **7.** Making an advertisement is a long and difficult **process**.

_____ **8.** When kids want to communicate with others, they can quickly **spread** information through chat rooms and instant messaging.

LISTENING

Critical Thinking Strategy

Guessing the Main Idea

Sometimes speakers clearly give the main idea of a presentation or lecture. But in an informal conversation or an interview, they do not always give the main idea. In this situation, you need to **add up** (put together) all the details to guess the main idea.

A. LISTENING FOR THE MAIN IDEA Listen to the radio interview. As you listen, try to answer this question:
• What does Tina Lane's company do with information?

B. LISTENING FOR DETAILS Listen again. Listen for the answers to these questions. Check (✓) the correct answers. Each question may have more than one correct answer.

1. Who does Tina sell information to?

   _____ companies that manufacture products   _____ advertisers

   _____ trend setters

2. Why does Tina get information from kids?

   _____ Kids go to shopping malls.   _____ Kids begin trends.

3. Where does Tina find kids to hire?

   _____ malls   _____ high schools   _____ music places

   _____ clothing stores   _____ parks

4. What does Tina do with the information?

   _____ puts it in a database   _____ gives it back to the kids

   _____ sees what pops out from the information

5. What kind of technology is important these days?

   _____ Walkman   _____ laptops   _____ portable technology

   _____ iPods   _____ cell phones

Listening Strategy

Listening for Reasons

When listening to an interview, presentation, or lecture, it's important to listen for reasons. Speakers answer the question *Why* with a reason. Listen for phrases such as *one reason is that* and *because*.

Example: Many advertisements target teenagers and young adults. **One reason is that** young consumers are especially interested in new products. Teenagers often buy a trendy new item **because** they want to conform—be like everyone else.

C. LISTENING FOR REASONS Listen to the end of the interview again. Write the answer to this question on the lines: Why is technology important to businesses these days?

_____

_____

_____

AFTER LISTENING

A. DISCUSSING THE INTERVIEW Look at your answers in Activities B and C (pages 90-91). In small groups, compare your answers. Then write _one_ sentence to answer the main idea question:
• What does Tina Lane's company do with information?

_____

_____

B. COMPARING IDEAS Each group will put its sentence about the main idea on the board. Are the sentences similar? Decide which sentence you like most.

C. MAKING CONNECTIONS For this activity, you are a group of advertisers. Here is your job: you need to write a magazine ad for one specific product. Follow these steps.

1. Go back and choose one trend from your survey on page 81.

2. Think of a good product that this trend leads you to. It can be anything: a clothing style, a type of car, a kind of food, a piece of technology, etc.

3. Design an ad to fill one magazine page. Include:
   • a piece of art (a photo or drawing)
   • the name of the product
   • reason(s) to buy this product

4. Share your ad with the class.

PART ⑤ ACADEMIC ENGLISH
Thinking Critically about College Finances

BEFORE LISTENING

Credit cards

👥 **A. BRAINSTORMING** You are going to hear a lecture in a business class. Before you listen, answer these questions with a partner.

1. What are some advantages of credit cards? What are some disadvantages of credit cards?

2. What advice can you give people about their first credit card?

3. Why are credit cards sometimes dangerous?

👥 **B. THINKING AHEAD** What are some cultural **values**—ideas about what is important—in your culture? For each value in the chart, decide if your culture thinks it is good or bad (or possibly both good *and* bad). Check (✓) your answers. Then, in small groups, compare your answers.

Values	Good	Bad	Both
Education			
Financial success			
Honesty (telling the truth)			
Giving to poor people			
Doing what is right, even when this is difficult			
Physical beauty			
Greed (wanting much more money than one needs)			
Hard work			
Working with other people			
Independence (not needing other people)			

C. VOCABULARY PREPARATION Read the sentences below. The words and phrases in blue are from the lecture. Match the definitions in the box with the words and phrases in blue. Write the correct letters on the lines.

> a. %
> b. beauty
> c. money that you pay to borrow money
> d. needing to pay back money
> e. a system of buying now and paying later

_____e_____ **1.** My father always said, "Be careful about **credit**. It can get you in big financial trouble."

_____ **2.** What **percent** of college students borrow money for books and tuition?

_____ **3.** My credit card has an **interest rate** of 20%. Does this seem high to you?

_____ **4.** Terry borrowed money from the bank. Now she's worried that she will be **in debt** for a long time.

_____ **5.** What's more important—physical **attractiveness** or inner goodness (doing what is right)?

D. VOCABULARY CHECK Look at the chart in Activity B. Write definitions for the words on the lines.

honesty = _____

greed = _____

independence = _____

LISTENING

Listening Strategy

Listening for the Topic

Often a speaker will clearly say the main topic at the beginning of a lecture or presentation. When listening for the topic, listen for phrases such as *Today I'm going to talk about . . .; In today's lecture, I'll explore . . .;* and *Today we're going to learn about . . . .*

Examples: Hello class. **Today I'm going to talk** about personal finance. To begin . . .

All right, let's get started. **In today's lecture, I'll explore** the dangers of credit cards.

Good morning. **Today we're going to learn about** trends and trend spotters.

A. LISTENING FOR THE TOPIC Listen to Section 1 of the lecture. As you listen, fill in the graphic organizer below. Write the topic of the lecture in the top box. Then write the two areas that the professor will explore in the other boxes.

Topic

Area 1

Area 2

Listening Strategy

Knowing When to Take Notes

Professors often give lectures. It's important for you to take notes—write down information—as you listen. Taking notes can be difficult because you have to listen and write at the same time. Here are some suggestions for taking good notes.

1. Don't try to write everything that the professor says. It's not possible.

2. Copy everything that the professor writes on the board.

3. Take notes when the professor:
   • seems to get excited
   • repeats something
   • speaks very slowly
   • gives a definition of a word

B. LISTENING FOR DETAILS Listen to Section 2 of the lecture. In the box below, write anything important that the professor says. Also, add the definition of one word. (Hint: Listen for the expression *in other words*.)

Definition:

Using a T-Chart

In Chapter 2, you learned to use a graphic organizer. There are many kinds of graphic organizers. One is a T-chart. It's called a T-chart because its shape is like the letter T. It is good to take notes on a T-chart if there is a list of:
- things to do and things *not* to do (Dos and Don'ts)
- advantages (or disadvantages) of two things
- differences between two things

 C. LISTENING FOR DETAILS Listen to Section 3 of the lecture. Take notes on the T-chart below. Also, add three definitions to the box below.

Dos	Don'ts

Vocabulary

shop around =

introductory rates =

pay off the balance =

D. LISTENING FOR DETAILS Listen to Section 4 of the lecture. As you listen, answer these questions:

1. What *don't* most companies do?

_____

_____

2. What *do* most companies do?

_____

_____

Now use the T-chart to compare values and ads.

Values	Ads

E. COMPARING NOTES Compare your notes with a partner's. Do you agree on what is important? Why did you include this information? (Look again at the list in the Listening Strategy box on page 94.)

AFTER LISTENING

Speaking Strategy

Expressing an Opinion

A professor often asks students for their opinions. To express an opinion, begin by saying *I think; It seems to me that; I don't think;* or *It doesn't seem to me that.*

Examples: **I think** credit cards are dangerous. You can charge a lot and then not have enough money to pay your credit card bill.

It doesn't seem to me that credit cards are dangerous. They make it much easier to buy things. You just need to be careful.

EXPRESSING OPINIONS In small groups, discuss these questions. Give your opinions.

1. Do you have any credit cards? What do you think about the professor's advice about them? Can you give more suggestions?

2. On page 92 there is a list of some values. What are three important values to you? (You can use values on this list or other values.)

3. Is there a difference between an *ideal* value and what people really do? (For example, maybe honesty is an important value, but it is an *ideal*. Most people sometimes tell "small" lies for social reasons, to be polite.)

PUT IT ALL TOGETHER

 A. CHOOSING AN AD TO DISCUSS Look on the Internet or in magazines to find an interesting ad. (Try to find an ad that shows some new trend.) When you find an interesting ad, answer the questions in the chart.

What product is the company advertising?	
What age group does the ad appeal to?	
What trend do you see in the ad?	
What value does the ad say is important?	
Is this value the same as a cultural value or different from it?	
Does the ad make you want to buy the product? Why or why not?	

B. SHARING WHAT YOU LEARNED Bring the ad and your chart to class. In small groups, share the ad and talk about it. Make a list of the trends and values in your group's ads.

UNIT ② VOCABULARY WORKSHOP

Review vocabulary that you learned in Chapters 3 and 4.

A. MATCHING Match the words on the left with the definitions on the right. Write the correct letters on the lines.

_g_	**1.** actually	**a.**	ability
_____	**2.** aptitude	**b.**	bad point or characteristic
_____	**3.** data	**c.**	choose
_____	**4.** disadvantage	**d.**	give someone a job
_____	**5.** greed	**e.**	information
_____	**6.** hire	**f.**	shopping center
_____	**7.** mall	**g.**	really; in fact
_____	**8.** pick	**h.**	say "no"
_____	**9.** refuse	**i.**	things
_____	**10.** stuff	**j.**	wanting much more than you need

B. TRUE OR FALSE? Which sentences are true? Which sentences are false? Fill in T for *True* or F for *False*.

1. Cell phones and computers are examples of **technology**.　　(T)　　(F)

2. If you **pay off** a loan, you pay only the interest.　　(T)　　(F)

3. If you **owe** someone money, you need to pay them.　　(T)　　(F)

4. You cannot easily move something **portable**.　　(T)　　(F)

5. An **internship** can lead to a good job.　　(T)　　(F)

6. If you want to be careful with your money, it's a good idea to begin with a **budget**.　　(T)　　(F)

7. If you have to **support yourself**, you need to have a job.　　(T)　　(F)

8. You probably don't want to take a **fabulous** class.　　(T)　　(F)

C. HIGH FREQUENCY WORDS In the box below are some of the most common words in English. Fill in the blanks with words from the box. When you finish, check your answers in the reading on page 77.

apply	college	cover	~~introductory~~	saving
both	complete	exercises	material	

Course Description

This is a(n) _____introductory_____ class in personal finance. You will
                         1

learn to _____ basic financial ideas to your own spending,
                    2

_____, and investing habits. You will work on *critical thinking*—your
           3

ability to use logic and solve problems. You will need to use critical thinking skills in this class and in

most of your classes in _____.
                              4

Course Requirements

You cannot be absent more than four times in the semester. There will be six quizzes on the

_____ in the textbook. There will also be a midterm exam and a final exam.
         5

These exams will _____ material from _____ the
                          6   7

textbook and the lectures in class. In addition, you must _____ five critical
                                                                  8

thinking _____.
              9

SOCIOLOGY

CHAPTER 5

Connecting with Others

Discuss these questions:
- Look at the picture. Where are the people?
- What are some good ways to meet people?
- What do you like to do with your friends?
- Read the chapter title. What do you think the chapter will be about?

PART ① INTRODUCTION Making Friends

A. THINKING AHEAD Discuss these questions with a partner.

1. What is a *friend*? Complete this sentence:

   A friend is someone who _____.

2. Why do people need friends?

3. How do people usually find friends?

B. READING: A WEBSITE Friendsconnect.net is a website. It helps people meet and communicate with friends. It also has useful information about friendship. For example, *Ask Trish* answers questions about making and keeping friends.

Read the webpage on page 105. As you read, think about this question:
• Do you agree with Trish?

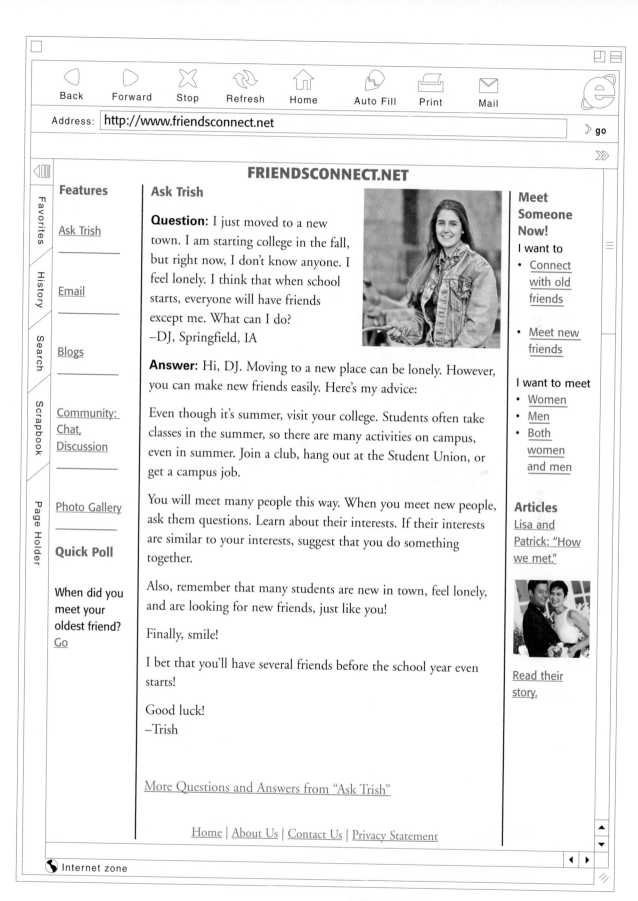

FRIENDSCONNECT.NET

Features

Ask Trish

_____

Email

_____

Blogs

_____

Community:
Chat,
Discussion

_____

Photo Gallery

_____

Quick Poll

When did you
meet your
oldest friend?
Go

Ask Trish

Question: I just moved to a new town. I am starting college in the fall, but right now, I don't know anyone. I feel lonely. I think that when school starts, everyone will have friends except me. What can I do?
–DJ, Springfield, IA

Answer: Hi, DJ. Moving to a new place can be lonely. However, you can make new friends easily. Here's my advice:

Even though it's summer, visit your college. Students often take classes in the summer, so there are many activities on campus, even in summer. Join a club, hang out at the Student Union, or get a campus job.

You will meet many people this way. When you meet new people, ask them questions. Learn about their interests. If their interests are similar to your interests, suggest that you do something together.

Also, remember that many students are new in town, feel lonely, and are looking for new friends, just like you!

Finally, smile!

I bet that you'll have several friends before the school year even starts!

Good luck!
–Trish

More Questions and Answers from "Ask Trish"

Home | About Us | Contact Us | Privacy Statement

Meet Someone Now!

I want to
- Connect with old friends

- Meet new friends

I want to meet
- Women
- Men
- Both women and men

Articles
Lisa and Patrick: "How we met."

Read their story.

Internet zone

Critical Thinking Strategy

Responding to Information on the Internet

Information on the Internet is not always correct. Sometimes the information is just wrong. Other times the information is the author's opinion, and you may or may not agree with it. It's important to think about information on the Internet and decide for yourself if it's correct.

C. RESPONDING TO INFORMATION ON THE INTERNET Discuss these questions with a partner.

1. Is the information on the webpage on page 105 correct, in your opinion? What is correct? What isn't correct?

2. Do you agree with Trish's advice? Explain your answer.

3. Read the questions below. Write your answers in the chart. Then ask your partner the questions. Write your partner's answers in the chart. Compare your answers.

Questions	My Answers	My Partner's Answers
Who are your oldest friends? How did you meet?		
What do you and your friends do together?		
What do you and your friends talk about?		
How do you and your friends **stay in touch** (communicate)—for example, by phone or by email?		
Do you **do favors for** (help) your friends? Do they do favors for you? Give an example.		
If you have a serious problem, do you talk to a friend or someone else like a family member?		
What's the best way to meet new people?		

D. JOURNAL WRITING Choose one of the topics below. Write about it for five minutes. Don't worry about grammar. Don't use a dictionary.

• The best way to make new friends is to . . .

• It is hard to stay in touch with . . .

PART ② SOCIAL LANGUAGE How Do *You* Like to Meet People?

BEFORE LISTENING

A barbecue

A classroom

A math club

A. THINKING AHEAD Look at the pictures. Discuss each situation with a partner. Are these good places to meet new people? Why or why not?

B. VOCABULARY PREPARATION Read the sentences below. The expressions in blue are from the conversation. Match them with the definitions in the box. Write the correct letters on the lines.

> a. become friends with people
> b. I don't know what will happen, but I'll probably have a good time.
> c. meet with and do something
> d. shared a lot of the same interests
> e. There are many people doing a lot of different things.

____a____ **1.** Sometimes it's hard to **get to know people** in a new place.

_____ **2.** Ashley and Viktor both liked biology, and they both liked golf. They **had a lot in common**.

_____ **3.** Mike might **get together** with someone in his study group.

_____ **4.** Rachel really likes big groups because **there's a lot going on**.

_____ **5.** Rachel said: "I don't know anyone at the party, but I'm going anyway. **I'll take my chances**."

LISTENING

A. LISTENING FOR MAIN IDEAS Listen to the conversation. As you listen, fill in the correct bubbles.

1. What event is happening tonight?

ⓐ a dance   ⓑ a barbecue   ⓒ a biology club meeting

2. Who is definitely going to the event?

ⓐ Ashley   ⓑ Rachel   ⓒ Mike

B. LISTENING FOR DETAILS Listen to the conversation again. Listen for different ways to meet people. What are the advantages of each one? Make notes in the chart below.

Ways to Meet People	Advantages
big parties	a lot of people; a lot of possibilities for meeting people

Listening Strategy

Listening for Opinions

Opinions are a person's ideas or feelings. Opinions are not right or wrong. They are only *one* person's ideas or feelings. Another person may think or feel differently. Opinions often follow expressions such as *I think (that)*, *I don't think (that)*, and *If you ask me*.

Examples: **I think that** it is hard to meet new people. I'm very shy.
I don't think that it is hard to meet new people. You just need to start a conversation.
If you ask me, meeting new people is easy. Everyone here is so nice.

C. LISTENING FOR OPINIONS Listen to the conversation again. Listen for opinions about the best way to meet people. Match the opinions with the speakers. Write the correct letters on the lines.

Speakers

_____ Rachel

_____ Mike

_____ Ashley

Opinions

a. thinks classes or small groups are the best way to meet people

b. thinks parties and big groups are the best way to meet people

c. thinks campus clubs are the best way to meet people

AFTER LISTENING

A. TAKING A SURVEY Talk to two classmates. Ask them about meeting people. Write their answers in the chart below.

Example:
A: Do you think that it's difficult to meet people here?
B: No.
A: Why not?
B: Because there are a lot of interesting people here.

Questions	Examples	Classmate 1	Classmate 2
1. Do you think that it's difficult to meet people at school?	☐ Yes ☑ No	☐ Yes ☐ No	☐ Yes ☐ No
2. Why or why not?	interesting people here		
3. What do you think is the best way to meet new people?	parties		
4. Why is this the best way?	a lot of people in one place		

B. DISCUSSING SURVEY RESULTS In small groups, discuss the results of your survey. Answer these questions.

1. How did most people answer Question 1? What reasons did they give?

2. What ways do your classmates like to meet people?

3. Is there a difference between female classmates' answers and male classmates' answers? If so, give examples. Are there any differences in the answers of classmates from different cultures?

PART ③ THE MECHANICS OF LISTENING AND SPEAKING

PRONUNCIATION

> ### 🎧 Reduced Forms of Words with /t/ and /y/
>
> When people speak quickly, words become reduced so that two or three words sound like one word. When /y/ follows /t/, they sometimes sound like /ch/. Here are some examples.
>
> **Examples:**
>
> | | Long Form | | Reduced Form |
> |---|---|---|---|
> | | **Don't you** want to dance? | → | **Doncha** want to dance? |
> | | How **about you**? | → | How **boutchu**? |
> | | Why **aren't you** going? | → | Why **arenchu** going? |
> | | Why **didn't you** go? | → | Why **dinchu** go? |
> | | I **want you** to meet someone. | → | I **wanchu** to meet someone. |

🎧 **A. REDUCED FORMS OF WORDS WITH /t/ AND /y/** Listen to the sentences. You are going to hear the reduced form of some words. Write the long forms on the lines.

1. _____*Don't you*_____ want to meet some new people?

2. Why _____ going to the barbecue?

3. I like the new English teacher. How _____?

4. Ashley, I _____ to meet someone. This is Viktor.

5. The party was fun. Why _____ go?

WORDS IN PHRASES

> ### It's easy/hard + Infinitive
>
> Here are some phrases with *It's easy/hard* + infinitive (to + the simple form of a verb). You can use them to give an opinion about meeting people.
>
> **Examples:**   **It's easy to meet** people at City College.
>   **It's hard to stay in touch** with my family.

👥 **B. WORDS IN PHRASES** Look at the survey on meeting people on page 110. With a partner, talk about the easy ways and the hard ways to meet people. Use *It's hard/easy* + infinitive.

LANGUAGE FUNCTIONS

Giving an Opinion

When you give an opinion, you want to make sure you say that the idea or feeling is only *your* idea or feeling. You learned on page 109 that three expressions for giving an opinion are *I think (that)*, *I don't think (that)*, and *If you ask me.*

Examples: **I think that** the International Students' Club is great.
I don't think that I will have time to join a club.
If you ask me, you should join a club.

C. GIVING AN OPINION Listen to the sentences. Write the expressions that you hear on the lines.

1. _____ I think that _____ campus clubs are the best way to meet people.

2. _____, it's hard to get to know people around here.

3. _____ small groups are the best way to meet people.

4. _____, campus clubs are really fun.

5. _____ you will meet some nice people in your computer class.

6. _____ you should go to a movie on a first date.

Asking for an Opinion

Sometimes you want to ask people for their opinions. Often you ask for an opinion after you give your own opinion. Here are some expressions:

How about you?
What about you?
What do you think?
Don't you think?*

Example: **A:** I think clubs are fun. **How about you?**
B: Yes, I'm in the International Students' Club. It's great.

*When people use the question *Don't you think?* they expect the answer to be "Yes."

D. ASKING FOR AN OPINION Listen to the sentences. Write the expressions that you hear on the lines.

1. I like big parties. _____ How about you _____?

2. I don't like big groups. _____?

3. Campus clubs are a good way to meet people. _____?

4. _____ a barbecue is the best way to get to know someone?

5. I don't like big parties. _____ ?

6. Study groups are a good way to meet interesting people. _____ ?

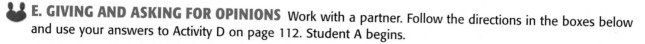 **E. GIVING AND ASKING FOR OPINIONS** Work with a partner. Follow the directions in the boxes below and use your answers to Activity D on page 112. Student A begins.

Example: **A:** I like big parties. How about you?
   B: I like them a lot.
   A: Why?
   B: They're a good way to meet people.

Student A

Read Number 1 from Activity D to your partner.

Listen to your partner's answer. Ask *Why?* if your partner's answer is positive. Ask *Why not?* if your partner's answer is negative. Listen to your partner's answer.

Listen to your partner read Number 2 from Activity D. Give an opinion in response to your partner's question.

Listen to your partner's question. Give a reason for your opinion.

Repeat for Numbers 3–6 from Activity D.

Student B

Listen to your partner read Number 1 from Activity D. Give an opinion in response to your partner's question.

Listen to your partner's question. Give a reason for your opinion.

Then read Number 2 from Activity D to your partner.

Listen to your partner's answer. Ask *Why?* if your partner's answer is positive. Ask *Why not?* if your partner's answer is negative. Listen to your partner's answer.

Repeat for Numbers 3–6 from Activity D.

PUT IT TOGETHER

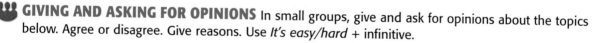 **GIVING AND ASKING FOR OPINIONS** In small groups, give and ask for opinions about the topics below. Agree or disagree. Give reasons. Use *It's easy/hard* + infinitive.

• the best place to go or the best thing to do with a new friend
• the best way to meet new friends
• big parties
• study groups

Example: **A:** I think a movie is the best place to go with a new friend. What about you?
   B: I disagree. It's hard to talk at a movie.
   C: That's true, but you can talk after the movie. You can talk *about* the movie.

PART ④ BROADCAST ENGLISH Pen Pals

BEFORE LISTENING

Critical Thinking Strategy

Thinking Ahead

Often you know the topic of something that you are going to listen to before you listen to it. When you know the topic, think about it before you listen. Ask yourself questions about it. That way, you will be better prepared to listen.

A. THINKING AHEAD You are going to hear a radio interview with two people who **lost touch with** (stopped communicating with) each other. They wrote to each other for a long time and then stopped writing. Many years later, they found each other again.

Answer the questions in the chart below. Then write a question in the chart. Ask your partner the questions. Write your partner's answers in the chart. Compare answers.

Questions	My Answers	My Partner's Answers
If you lose touch with someone, what are some ways to find him or her again?		
Did you lose touch with someone? If yes, who? What happened?		
Your question:		

B. VOCABULARY PREPARATION Read the sentences below. The words in blue are from the radio interview. Match the words in blue with the definitions in the box. Write the correct letters on the lines.

a. begin doing again	f. people who write to each other, usually from far away
~~b.~~ a board game with two players	
c. informal language	g. planned
d. looked	h. sent on to another address
e. met again after being separated	i. social appointment or meeting
	j. very special and amazing qualities

_____b_____ **1.** Viktor is an excellent **chess** player.

_____ **2.** Viktor and Ashley **set up** a meeting of the Chess Club.

_____ **3.** I stopped playing chess when I left school, but now I might **get back into** it.

_____ **4.** I have a **date** to play golf with Linda next week.

_____ **5.** Rachel and Min are **pen pals**. They started writing to each other when they were children.

_____ **6.** Rachel moved to a new apartment, and the post office **forwarded** Min's letters to her.

_____ **7.** American **slang** is sometimes difficult for English learners.

_____ **8.** I **reunited with** Michel after 15 years.

_____ **9. A:** How did you find your old friend?
      B: It was possible because of the **wonders** of the Internet! You can find out all kinds of things on the Internet.

_____ **10. A:** How did you find your friend on the Internet?
      B: I **did a search** for his name. I put "Michel Lachappelle" in the Google search box.

LISTENING

Alexi

Lydia

🎧 **A. LISTENING FOR MAIN IDEAS** Read the questions. Then listen to the interview. Answer the questions while you listen. Write your answers on the lines.

1. Why did Lydia write to Alexi?

_____

2. How did Lydia and Alexi lose touch?

_____

3. How did Lydia and Alexi reunite?

_____

🎧 **B. LISTENING FOR DETAILS** Listen again. Listen for the answers to these questions. Check (✓) the correct answers.

1. When they became pen pals, Lydia was _____.

_____ a teenager   _____ 12 years old   _____ 10 years old

2. Alexi thought that writing to Lydia was a good way to practice _____.

_____ chess playing   _____ English   _____ writing

3. What didn't Lydia and Alexi talk about in their letters?

_____ music   _____ chess   _____ school

4. When Lydia found Alexi, he was a graduate student in _____ in the U.S.

_____ mathematics   _____ computer science   _____ English

Guessing the Meaning from Context

You can often guess the meanings of new words or expressions when they are similar to words or expressions that you already know.

Example: **You know:** to hang out means to spend time ➔ **You hear:** There's a great new hangout at the mall. ➔ **You can guess:** *a* hangout is a place *to* hang out

C. GUESSING THE MEANING FROM CONTEXT Listen to part of the interview. You will hear two new expressions. You already know the expression *lose touch*. What do these two expressions mean? Write the correct letters on the lines.

_____ **1.** get back in touch

_____ **2.** stay in touch

a. continue to communicate

b. start communicating again after stopping

AFTER LISTENING

A. DISCUSSING THE INTERVIEW Is it always a good thing to find an old friend? In small groups, discuss the advantages and disadvantages of reuniting with an old friend. Write your ideas in the T-chart.

Getting Back in Touch

Advantages	Disadvantages

 B. MAKING CONNECTIONS Do an Internet search for an old friend. Type the person's name into the search box on www.google.com. Put quotation marks (" ") around the name. (This way, you have fewer results.) What happened? Take notes on your search experience.

C. SHARING YOUR EXPERIENCE In small groups, discuss your Internet search experience. Did you find your friend? If yes, did you get in touch with him or her? Why or why not?

BEFORE LISTENING

A. THINKING AHEAD You are going to hear a presentation about campus clubs. Most American colleges and universities have campus clubs. There are different types of clubs for different students' interests. Some types include:

- academic (related to school)
- professional (related to jobs and professions)
- service (related to helping people)
- general interest (related to hobbies, interests, or free-time activities)

What kinds of interests do college students have? What do they study? What do they do for fun? With a partner, fill in the chart with five examples in each category.

Academic	Professional	Service	General Interest
biology	business careers	environment	cooking

B. VOCABULARY PREPARATION Read the sentences on page 119. The words and phrases in blue are from the presentation. Match the definitions in the box with the words in blue. Write the correct letters on the lines.

a. are active; do things
b. are members of
c. leave; stop going to
d. moved from one place to another
e. practice with managing people and organizations
f. someone in the third year of college in the United States
g. useful, practical

_____*g*_____ **1.** You can get **real-world** experience at the business club. For example, you can learn how to start a business.

_____ **2.** Hector is getting **leadership experience** at the computer club. He's the vice president.

_____ **3.** Maria's mother said, "Don't **drop out** of college. Please stay until you graduate."

_____ **4.** Maria missed her mother, so she **transferred** to a college near home.

_____ **5.** Rachel and Danielle **belong to** the drama club. They enjoy acting and reading plays.

_____ **6.** We don't just talk! We **take action**!

_____ **7.** Megan is a **junior** at City College. Next year, she'll graduate.

LISTENING

A. LISTENING FOR THE MAIN IDEA Listen to the presentation. As you listen, try to answer this question:
• What are some advantages of campus clubs?

Listening Strategy

Organizing Your Notes

A chart is one way to organize your notes. Decide on an organizational pattern and make a grid to match it. For example, if a presentation has four speakers, make a grid with four main sections. An example of this type of grid is on page 120.

B. LISTENING FOR DETAILS The presentation has four speakers. Use the chart to take notes on each speaker's information. First, listen only for the speaker's job or title. Write the job or title in the correct box.

Speakers	Jobs and Titles	Main Ideas	Details
Speaker 1: Danielle	Moderator	Reasons to join clubs	
Speaker 2: Viktor			Not just for biology majors. They read and talk about biology. They go on field trips. They have guest speakers.
Speaker 3: Ashley		The purpose of the international business club	
Speaker 4: Winston	Vice president of the environment club		

Listen again. Listen for the main idea of each speaker's presentation. Write your notes in the *Main Ideas* column.

Listen one more time. Listen for details that each speaker gives. Write your notes in the *Details* column.

C. CHECKING YOUR NOTES Listen to the presentation. Check your notes. Then compare your notes with a partner's notes.

AFTER LISTENING

A. MAKING CONNECTIONS In small groups, think about the presentation. Match the students below with the clubs in the box. There may be more than one club for each student.

a. biology club	b. environment club	c. international business club

_____ **1.** Maria is a business major. She wants an internship this summer.

_____ **2.** Ivan is a computer science major, but he enjoyed science in high school.

_____ **3.** Rachel likes working with children, and she's concerned about pollution.

_____ **4.** Adam is studying Japanese. He wants to work for a Japanese company someday.

_____ **5.** Susan is a biology major, and she wants to meet some new people.

B. DISCUSSION In small groups, discuss these questions.

1. Do you belong to a club?

2. If you belong to a club, what kind? Why do you belong to this club? If you do not belong to a club, why not?

PUT IT ALL TOGETHER

A. DOING RESEARCH Go to the website for a college or university. You can go to the website of one of the schools below or to any school that you are interested in.

• Miami Dade College (USA)
• Lansing Community College (USA)
• San Diego State University (USA)
• Rutgers University (USA)
• The University of Toronto (Canada)
• University of Buckingham (England)

B. EXPLORING THE WEBSITE Go to the website of the school that you chose in Activity A. Do a search for "student organizations," "campus clubs," "student groups," or "student activities." Find information about five clubs. Write the information on the chart on page 122.

Name of School: _____

Clubs	Purposes of Clubs or Examples of Club Activities

Speaking Strategy

Making Eye Contact

Make eye contact with (look at) people when you speak to them. If you are using notes, look at your notes quickly and then look up. If you are talking to a group, move your eyes from person to person. This helps people to pay attention to you.

C. SHARING WHAT YOU LEARNED In small groups, discuss what you learned. Remember to make eye contact as you speak. Then discuss the questions below.

1. What schools had the most clubs or the most interesting clubs?

2. Of all the clubs, which one seems the most unusual?

3. Of all the clubs, which one seems the most interesting?

CHAPTER 6

Sports and Life

Discuss these questions:

- Look at the picture. What are the people doing?
- Do you think this is a fun activity? Explain your answer.
- What is your favorite way to exercise? Why?
- Read the chapter title. What do you think the chapter will be about?

PART ① INTRODUCTION College Sports

1. _____   3. _____   5. _____

2. _____   4. _____   6. _____

A. THINKING AHEAD Look at the pictures and discuss these questions with a partner.

1. What sports are the students doing? Match the pictures with the sports. Write the correct letters on the lines below the pictures.

    a. baseball*   **c.** softball*   **e.** track and field

    b. basketball   **d.** swimming   **f.** volleyball

2. Do you **participate in** (do or play) any of these sports? Which ones?

3. Do you like to watch other people do any of these sports? Which ones?

*Men usually play baseball. Women usually play softball.

B. READING: AN ATHLETIC CALENDAR College calendars show academic and non-academic information. Non-academic information might include events and activities for students. One kind of non-academic calendar at some colleges lists the **athletic** (sports) events on campus.

Read the calendar below. It lists the **intercollegiate athletic events** (competitive sports events with other schools) at City College. As you read, think about these questions.

1. Do men's and women's teams play games with the same colleges?

2. In this month, which team has the most games?

3. Why might school teams play these sports in March (in the spring)?

4. What sports might school teams play in the fall or winter?

College Athletics • Intercollegiate Events • March

Sunday	Monday	Tuesday	Wednesday	Thursday	Friday	Saturday
		1 Baseball vs. Bay College	**2**	**3**	**4** Women's Basketball vs. Greenhill College	**5** Men's Basketball vs. Greenhill College
6 Softball vs. Western State College	**7**	**8**	**9**	**10**	**11** Baseball vs. Eastern State College	**12** Women's Volleyball vs. Valley College
13 Men's Volleyball vs. Valley College	**14**	**15** Women's Swimming vs. Southern State College	**16** Men's Swimming vs. Southern State College	**17**	**18**	**19**
20 Women's Volleyball vs. Branson College	**21** Men's Volleyball vs. Branson College	**22**	**23**	**24** Softball vs. Carlmont College	**25**	**26** Track and Field **Invitational** (event)
27	**28** Baseball vs. Carlmont College	**29**	**30** Baseball vs. Carlmont College	**31**		

C. TALKING ABOUT IT Talk about sports. First, read the questions and write your answers in the chart. Then ask a partner the questions. Write your partner's answers. Compare your answers.

Questions	My Answers	My Partner's Answers
Are sports important? Why or why not?		
Do you play any sports? Which ones?		
Do you like team sports (for example, soccer) or individual sports (for example, running)?		
Are you competitive? Why or why not?		
Is exercise important? Why or why not?		
How do you **stay fit** (stay in good physical condition)?		

D. JOURNAL WRITING Choose *one* of these topics. Write about it for five minutes. Don't worry about grammar. Don't use a dictionary.

• I like team sports/individual sports because . . .
• I don't like team sports because . . .
• Exercise is important because . . .
• I don't like to exercise because . . .

PART ② SOCIAL LANGUAGE Why Do You Play or Watch Sports?

BEFORE LISTENING

Skateboarding

Snowboarding

Surfing

A. THINKING AHEAD You are going to listen to people discuss why they play or watch sports. What are some reasons to play sports? What are some reasons to watch sports? In small groups, brainstorm reasons why people like to play sports and why people like to watch sports. One person in the group should write down your answers.

B. VOCABULARY PREPARATION Read the sentences below. The words and phrases in blue are from the interviews. Match the definitions in the box with the words and phrases in blue. Write the correct letters on the lines.

a. clearly	f. exercise session
b. deciding; evaluating	g. manage and train
c. dangerous	h. a science; includes the study of movement
d. enjoys	i. should not
e. excitement	j. ways of living

_____ b ____ **1.** When Chris hits a golf ball, he is **judging** the distance between himself and the hole.

_____ **2.** Rafael enjoys the **thrills** of skateboarding. He thinks it's an exciting sport.

_____ **3.** Rafael **is into** skateboarding. He does it every day.

_____ **4.** I don't like skateboarding. It's too **risky**. I don't want to hurt myself.

_____ **5.** Mark is a **physics** major. He's interested in airplanes and space travel.

_____ **6.** You can get a good **workout** when you play tennis.

_____ **7.** If you like sports and children, why don't you **coach** a team?

_____ **8.** Mike has good **lifestyle habits**. He eats healthy food and exercises every day.

_____ **9.** Ashley **obviously** enjoys watching football: she never misses a game.

_____ **10.** You **are not supposed to** skateboard here. See the sign? It says "No Skateboarding."

LISTENING

A. LISTENING FOR THE MAIN IDEA Listen to the interviews. As you listen, try to answer this question:

• Do most of the people play a sport, or do they just watch sports on TV?

B. LISTENING FOR DETAILS Listen again and answer these questions.

1. What does Person 1 say? _____

_____

2. What does each person do? Match the activities in the box with the correct people below. Write the correct letters on the lines.

> **a. coaches a kid's soccer team**
> **b. plays basketball**
> **c. skateboards**
> **d. watches extreme sports on TV**
> **e. watches football on TV**

———— **1.** Person 2   ———— **3.** Person 4   ———— **5.** Person 6

———— **2.** Person 3   ———— **4.** Person 5

C. LISTENING FOR REASONS
Listen to parts of the interview. Listen for reasons. Match the people with the reasons. Write the correct letters on the lines.

———— **1.** Person 2   **a.** It's exciting, and it's a good workout.

———— **2.** Person 3   **b.** Sports are important for kids.

———— **3.** Person 4   **c.** It's relaxing.

———— **4.** Person 6   **d.** For the thrills.

Critical Thinking Strategy

Guessing the Meaning from General Context

In previous chapters, you used explanations, synonyms, examples, definitions, and familiar words to understand new words as you listen. Sometimes you don't have clues like these. Sometimes the context is more **general** (not specific). In this case, many words or sentences together give you information that helps you to guess new words.

D. GUESSING THE MEANING FROM GENERAL CONTEXT
Listen again. Guess the meanings of these informal expressions. Use the general context. Match the definitions with the expressions. Write the correct letters on the lines.

———— **1.** No way!   **a.** goodbye

———— **2.** Later.   **b.** a strong "no"

———— **3.** You bet.   **c.** a strong "yes"

AFTER LISTENING

👥 **A. TAKING A SURVEY** Talk to three classmates. Ask them the questions in the interview:

• Do you play any sports?
• Do you watch any sports?

Ask for reasons. Write their answers in the chart below.

Example: **A:** Do you play any sports?
               B: Yes, I play tennis.
               A: Why do you like to play tennis?
               B: It's a good workout.

Questions	Classmate 1	Classmate 2	Classmate 3
1. Do you play any sports? Which ones?	☐ Yes ☐ No	☐ Yes ☐ No	☐ Yes ☐ No
2. Why or why not?			
3. Do you watch any sports? Which ones?	☐ Yes ☐ No	☐ Yes ☐ No	☐ Yes ☐ No
4. Why or why not?			

👥 **B. DISCUSSING SURVEY RESULTS** In small groups, discuss the results of your survey. Answer these questions.

1. Do more people like to play sports or watch sports?

2. How many people do not play or watch sports?

3. What are people's reasons for:
   • playing sports
   • watching sports
   • not playing or watching sports

4. Is there a difference between female classmates' answers and male classmates' answers? If so, give examples. Are there any differences in the answers of classmates from different cultures?

PART ③ THE MECHANICS OF LISTENING AND SPEAKING

WORDS IN PHRASES

Play and *Go* + Names of Sports

Certain names of sports (such as *soccer* and *swimming*) follow the verbs *play* and *go*. Here are some examples:

I play	football.
	soccer.
	tennis.
	golf.
	basketball.
I go	swimming.
	running.
	hiking.

A. WORDS IN PHRASES Work with a partner. Look at the survey on sports on page 130. Which sports do you like to watch? Which sports do you like to participate in? Use the verbs above in complete sentences.

PRONUNCIATION

🎧 Reduced Forms of Words

When people speak quickly, some words become reduced, or shortened. One way that speakers shorten words is by **dropping** (not saying) the last sound.

Examples:	**Long Form**		**Reduced Form**
	I'm **doing** an interview.	→	I'm **doin'** an interview.
	I play soccer **and** basketball.	→	I play soccer **an'** basketball.

Another way speakers shorten words is by changing the vowel (*a, e, i, o,* or *u*) sound to *uh*.

| **Examples:** | I just like **to** play it. | → | I just like **tuh** play it. |
| | I'm **into** tennis. | → | I'm **intuh** tennis. |

B. REDUCED FORMS OF WORDS Listen to the sentences. You are going to hear the reduced forms of some words. Fill in the blanks with the long forms.

1. I like _____ tennis and golf.

2. Do you like _____ watch football _____ soccer

on TV?

3. I'm _____ my homework, and then I'm _____ TV.

4. I like _____ sports. I'm not _____

_____ sports.

5. I'm _____ _____ _____

_____.

/æ/ vs. /ɑ/

Some students have problems with the sounds /æ/ and /ɑ/. It might be difficult to hear the difference between these sounds, or it might be difficult to pronounce the difference. Listen to these words.

ad	→	odd		tap	→	top
hat	→	hot		backs	→	box
cat	→	cot		black	→	block
pat	→	pot		sack	→	sock
map	→	mop		racket	→	rocket

C. REPEATING WORDS WITH /æ/ AND /ɑ/ Listen again and repeat each word in the box above.

D. HEARING THE DIFFERENCE BETWEEN /æ/ AND /ɑ/ Circle the words that you hear.

1. hat   hot   **4.** racket   rocket   **7.** sack   sock

2. ad   odd   **5.** map   mop   **8.** cat   cot

3. backs   box   **6.** pat   pot   **9.** black   block

E. PRONOUNCING /æ/ AND /ɑ/ Work with a partner. First, Student A says one word in each pair. Student B circles that word. Then Student B says one word in each pair. Student A circles that word.

1. hat   hot   **4.** racket   rocket   **7.** sack   sock

2. ad   odd   **5.** map   mop   **8.** cat   cot

3. backs   box   **6.** pat   pot   **9.** black   block

F. PRONOUNCING /æ/ AND /ɑ/ IN SENTENCES Repeat each sentence after the speaker.

1. I saw an **odd ad**.

2. It's too **hot** to wear a **hat**.

3. He has the **packet** in his **pocket**.

4. Put your **sock** in the **sack**.

5. The black **cat** sat on top of the **cot**.

LANGUAGE FUNCTIONS

Refusing to Do Something

When you don't want to do something, you refuse (say *no*). Sometimes it's important to give a polite refusal; sometimes it doesn't matter. Here are some expressions for refusing:

Sorry.
No, thanks.
I'm sorry.
I'd rather not.
No way!

Which expressions are more polite? Which are less polite?

It's polite to give a reason for refusing.

Examples: **Sorry.** I'm in a hurry.
No, thanks, I don't have time.
I'm sorry. I'm too busy.
I'd rather not. I don't have the time.

G. REFUSING TO DO SOMETHING Work with a partner. Follow the directions in the boxes. Student B's box is on page 134. Take turns. Student A begins.

Example: **A:** May I ask you a question?
B: Sorry. I'm in a hurry.

Student A

Ask your partner for permission to do something from the following list:

1. to ask a question
2. to take your picture
3. to do the assignment with you
4. to work out with you

Then listen to your partner's request. Refuse politely and give a reason. Use expressions from the Language Functions box above.

Student B

Listen to your partner's request. Refuse politely and give a reason. Use expressions from the Language Functions box on page 133.

Then ask your partner for permission to do something from the following list:
1. to interview him or her for campus TV
2. to study with you tonight
3. to see his or her class notes
4. to play tennis with you

Asking for Explanations or Examples

When people give their opinions, sometimes you need more information to understand them. Asking for explanations or examples can help you understand opinions better.

Here are some expressions for asking for explanations or examples:

What do you mean?
What do you mean by that?   } for explanations
Why is that?
How come? (Why?)

Such as?   } for examples
Can you give me an example?

 H. ASKING FOR EXPLANATIONS OR EXAMPLES Work with a partner. Student A gives opinions about playing or watching sports. Student B asks for explanations or examples. Use the expressions above. Take turns.

Examples:
A: I think playing sports is good for children.
B: Why?
A: They can learn important skills.
B: Such as?
A: How to work with other people and how to be a leader.

B: I think extreme sports are risky.
A: What do you mean by that?
B: They're dangerous. People get hurt all the time.
A: Can you give me an example?
B: My brother broke his leg snowboarding last year.

PUT IT TOGETHER

FIND SOMEONE WHO Interview classmates and fill in the chart below. Follow these steps.

When you ask questions:
1. Ask for permission to ask questions.
2. Ask for an explanation or an example.
3. Ask for an opinion.
4. Ask *yes/no* questions with intonation going up at the end.
5. Ask *wh-* questions with intonation going down at the end.
6. Express understanding.
7. Keep the conversation going.

Find one person for each situation. When someone says *yes*, write his or her name in your chart. Ask for clarification or spelling when necessary. If someone says *no*, do not write his or her name in your chart.

When you answer questions:
1. Give permission using a reply that means *yes* or *maybe*.
2. For some answers, give an explanation or an example.
3. Give opinions for some answers.
4. Politely refuse to answer one question.
5. Use *like* or *enjoy*, *it's easy/hard*, and correct verbs with *sports* and names of sports.
6. Be prepared to repeat and clarify information.

Find Someone Who . . .	Name
plays soccer*	
watches sports on TV	
has an opinion about team sports	
has an unusual way to work out	
plays tennis	
has an opinion about extreme sports	
plays an unusual sport	
has a favorite movie about sports	

*In most countries what Americans call "soccer" is called "football".

Sporting Events—Problems and Solutions

BEFORE LISTENING

A sports fan

A. THINKING AHEAD In small groups, discuss large sporting events such as soccer, football, baseball, or hockey games. What are the **positive** (good) things about them? What are some of the **negative** (bad) things about them? Write your answers in the T-chart below.

Large Sporting Events

Positive Things	Negative Things

B. TALKING ABOUT IT The radio interview talks about the behavior of **fans** (people who support a team), **professional athletes** (the players), coaches, and **officials** (people who keep score at a game) at large sporting events. What do you know about the behavior of these groups at big games? In small groups, share your ideas.

C. VOCABULARY PREPARATION Read the sentences below. The words in blue are from the radio interview. Match the words in blue with the definitions in the box. Write the correct letters on the lines.

a. become close to	f. prevent
b. feel like a part of	g. not correct
c. a feeling of belonging to a group	h. make (someone) be quiet
d. give consequences for bad behavior	i. TV, radio, newspapers
e. have an effect on	j. wild and loud; not orderly

_____c_____ **1.** Sports can give people a **sense of community**. They enjoy being part of a big group of fans.

_____ **2.** It is **inappropriate** to break windows after a sports event.

_____ **3.** The player tried to **shut** the fan **up**.

_____ **4.** Fans often **identify with** a sports team; they feel like they are members of the team themselves.

_____ **5.** Sports can help people **form connections with** other fans.

_____ **6.** There was too much **rowdy** behavior at the event, and someone got hurt.

_____ **7.** The school should have more security guards to **discourage** bad behavior at sporting events.

_____ **8.** The manager is going to **punish** the player who started the fight.

_____ **9.** Representatives from the **media** interviewed both the players and the fans after yesterday's game.

_____ **10.** An excited crowd can sometimes **influence** people's actions.

LISTENING

Rowdy behavior at a sporting event

A. LISTENING FOR THE MAIN IDEA Listen to the radio interview. As you listen, try to answer this question:
- What problem about sporting events does Dr. Green discuss?

B. LISTENING FOR DETAILS Listen again. This time, listen for the answers to these questions. Fill in the correct bubbles.

1. Dr. Green is a(n) —————.

   Ⓐ physicist   Ⓑ athlete   Ⓒ psychologist

2. One problem area with sports is violence —————.

   Ⓐ on the field   Ⓑ before the game   Ⓒ at home

3. An example of "identifying with the team" is fans painting their ————— with team colors.

   Ⓐ cars   Ⓑ shirts   Ⓒ faces

4. Which is an example of violence that happens after a game?

   Ⓐ when a player tries to shut a fan up

   Ⓑ when a fan throws a bottle at a player

   Ⓒ when a fan burns a car

5. Which statement is true?

   Ⓐ Dr. Green thinks that colleges don't have problems with violence at games.

   Ⓑ Dr. Green thinks that the media has some responsibility for bad behavior at games.

   Ⓒ Dr. Green thinks that you cannot solve the problem of bad behavior at games.

Listening Strategy

Listening for Causes and Effects

When people are talking about problems, they often talk about the causes and the effects of the problems. It's important to understand the causes and the effects. Here are expressions that point out causes and/or effects:

X contributes to Y   X causes Y
(cause)   (effect)   (cause) (effect)

Y is the result of X
(effect)   (cause)

Example: For some students, too much **homework contributes to stress**.

C. LISTENING FOR CAUSES AND EFFECTS Listen to part of the radio interview. Listen for the causes of violence at games. Write three causes on the lines.

1. _____

2. _____

3. _____

Listening Strategy

Listening for Solutions to Problems

When people talk about problems, they often give solutions to them. It is important to listen for the solutions. Here are expressions that talk about solutions:

Is there any way to solve it?
Is there any solution?
What is the solution?
What can we do about it?

D. LISTENING FOR SOLUTIONS TO PROBLEMS Listen to part of the radio interview. Listen for the solutions to the problem of violence at games. Write four solutions on the lines below. Compare your answers with a partner's answers.

1. _____

2. _____

3. _____

4. _____

AFTER LISTENING

A. DISCUSSING THE INTERVIEW In small groups, discuss each of Dr. Green's solutions to the problem of violence at games.

B. EXPANSION In small groups, think of advice for professional athletes. What can they do to set a good example for the fans, especially for children? How would you like to see them behave? What would you like them to do? Write down your advice. Then share it with other groups.

C. EXTENSION Do an Internet search on a sports team. Are there any examples of violence at their recent games? In small groups, share your information.

PART ⑤ ACADEMIC ENGLISH Campus Athletics

BEFORE LISTENING

A. THINKING AHEAD You are going to hear a presentation about athletics at City College. Most American colleges have team sports. College teams play different sports in different seasons. Before you listen, make predictions with a partner. Answer the questions:

• What kinds of teams might colleges have?
• What sports do people play in each season—winter, spring, summer, and fall?

Then fill in the chart with examples in each category.

Seasons	Teams
Winter (Dec. 22–March 21)	basketball
Spring (March 22–June 21)	
Summer (June 22–Sept. 21)	
Fall (Sept. 22–Dec. 21)	

B. BRAINSTORMING What other kinds of physical activities or **facilities** (for example, a swimming pool) might a college have? For example, some students don't like playing on a team. What can they do at school to get a good workout? In small groups, brainstorm ideas.

C. VOCABULARY PREPARATION Read the sentences below. The words and phrases in blue are from the presentation. Match the definitions in the box with the words and phrases in blue. Write the correct letters on the lines.

> a. chance
> b. difficult
> c. for both men and women together
> d. a place to do sports and other physical activities
> e. places to keep things or to change clothes for working out
> f. purposes
> g. regularly
> h. rules
> ~~i.~~ sometimes

_____i_____ **1.** Rachel doesn't want to play on a team; she just wants to get a good workout **occasionally**.

_____ **2.** Rachel plans to go to the City College **Recreation Center** three times a week.

_____ **3.** Competition with a really good team can be **tough**; you have to play well to win.

_____ **4.** One of the Career Center's **goals** is to help students explore different careers.

_____ **5.** Playing on a team gives you the **opportunity** to learn leadership skills.

_____ **6.** City College has men's teams, women's teams, and **coed** teams.

_____ **7.** Mike likes to work out **on a regular basis**.

_____ **8.** If you want to play on a team, you must follow the **guidelines**.

_____ **9.** The **lockers** at the City College Recreation Center are ideal. They're very large and clean.

LISTENING

Playing badminton

Playing Frisbee

 A. LISTENING FOR MAIN IDEAS Listen to Section 1 of the presentation. As you listen, try to answer these questions:
- What is the speaker going to cover?
- What two types of sports activities are there at City College?

Listening Strategy

Using an Outline to Take Notes

An outline is one way to take notes on a presentation. An outline shows the organization of ideas in a presentation. When you use an outline to take notes, you can easily see the main idea, the supporting ideas, and the details in the presentation.

Here's an outline for the first part of the presentation on campus athletics at City College:

I. Sports and Recreation at City College
      A. Ways you can participate in sports
            1. teams
            2. Tiger Recreation Center
      B. Advantages of exercise
            1. reduces stress
            2. teamwork and leadership skills

Note: The information in "I" is the main idea of Section 1 of the presentation.

II. Intercollegiate teams

    A. Definition: intercollegiate teams compete with _____

    B. Winter and fall teams include

        1. *football* _____

        2. _____

        3. _____

        4. _____

        5. _____

    C. Spring teams include

        1. *baseball* _____

        2. _____

        3. _____

        4. _____

    D. Goals of intercollegiate athletics

        1. opportunity to form _____

        2. provide a sense of _____

    E. Students who want to participate

        1. must see an _____

        2. have a GPA of _____

🎧 **C. LISTENING FOR DETAILS** Listen to Section 3. As you listen, take notes.

III. Intramural teams

    A. Definition: Intramural teams play _____

    _____

    B. Team types

        1. *men's* _____

        2. _____

        3. _____

C. Sports include

1. basketball _____

2. _____

3. _____

4. _____

5. softball _____

6. _____

7. _____

8. _____

D. Students who want to participate must

1. follow _____

2. use _____

An aerobics class

A yoga class

D. CHECKING YOUR NOTES Listen to the entire presentation. Check your notes. In small groups, compare outlines.

AFTER LISTENING

Critical Thinking Strategy

Discussing Information in New Situations

Try to discuss information from a presentation or lecture immediately after you hear it. This will help you to understand and remember it better. When possible, try to meet with other students right after class to discuss what the professor said.

A. MAKING CONNECTIONS In small groups, read about the five students below. Then think about the presentation and use your notes. Match the students to the teams or places in the box. There may be more than one for each student.

a. an intercollegiate team	b. an intramural team	c. recreation center

___c___ **1.** Marc is not very competitive. He doesn't like teams, but he wants to get regular exercise.

_____ **2.** Ashley is very competitive. She was on her high school swim team.

_____ **3.** Emma isn't very competitive, but she enjoys being with other people, and she wants to learn how to play basketball.

_____ **4.** Mike likes to work out alone. He especially likes to swim.

_____ **5.** Sarah likes to play soccer occasionally, but she doesn't have the time to play regularly.

B. DISCUSSING In small groups, discuss this question.
• What do you do to stay healthy?

PUT IT ALL TOGETHER

 A. DOING RESEARCH Go to the website for a college or university. You can go to the website of one of the schools below or to any school that you are interested in.

- Notre Dame University (USA)
- University of California, Los Angeles (USA)
- University of Indiana, Bloomington (USA)
- University of Hawaii, Manoa (USA)
- University of Waterloo (Canada)
- University of the West of England (England)

 B. EXPLORING THE WEBSITE Go to the website of the school that you chose in Activity A. Search for "sports," "athletics," or "recreation opportunities." Answer the following questions about campus athletics.

- Does the college have intercollegiate athletics? What kinds of teams are there?
- What are the fall and winter sports? What are the spring sports? Who do they compete with?
- Does the college have intramural sports? If yes, which ones?
- Is there a recreation center for students? What facilities does it have?
- Are there guidelines for team players? Are there guidelines for the recreation center?

Take notes on the information that you find online.

Speaking Strategy

Giving and Getting Feedback

Feedback is helpful information about your work or presentation from other people. When you give a presentation, it's a good idea to get feedback from your listeners. You can get feedback from your teacher or from your classmates. When you give feedback, be positive and helpful. When you get feedback, think about ways to use the information the next time that you speak.

C. SHARING WHAT YOU LEARNED In small groups, present what you learned. Listen to your classmates' presentations. After each presentation, give the speaker feedback by discussing the questions below:

- Was the information complete?
- Was the information interesting?
- Did the speaker make eye contact?
- Did the speaker speak clearly?

UNIT 3 VOCABULARY WORKSHOP

Review vocabulary that you learned in Chapters 5 and 6.

A. MATCHING Match the words to the definitions. Write the correct letters on the lines.

_f_	**1.** coach	**a.** chance
____	**2.** drop out of	**b.** dangerous
____	**3.** goals	**c.** feel the same as
____	**4.** identify with	**d.** informal words
____	**5.** opportunity	**e.** leave; stop going to
____	**6.** real-world	**f.** manage a team and train players
____	**7.** risky	**g.** moved from one place to another
____	**8.** slang	**h.** purposes
____	**9.** transferred	**i.** special and amazing qualities
____	**10.** wonders	**j.** useful; practical

B. TRUE OR FALSE? Which sentences are true? Which sentences are false? Fill in T for *True* or F for *False*.

1. If a letter is **forwarded**, it's sent to a new address.   (T)   F

2. If you **get in touch with** someone, you stop communicating with him or her.   T   F

3. If you **have a lot in common** with someone, you are different from each other.   T   F

4. **Pen pals** are people who write to each other.   T   F

5. If you **are into** something, you don't like it very much.   T   F

6. If you do something **occasionally**, you do it every day.   T   F

7 Breaking windows is not an example of **inappropriate** behavior.   T   F

8. **Intercollegiate** teams play games with other colleges.   T   F

C. HIGH FREQUENCY WORDS In the boxes below are some of the most common words in English. Fill in the blanks with words from these boxes. When you finish, check your answers in the reading on page 105.

activities	feel	~~moved~~	starts
classes	friends	place	students

Question: I just _____ *moved* _____ to a new town. I am starting college in the fall, but
                                          1

right now, I don't know anyone. I _____ lonely. I think that when school
                                                         2

_____, everyone will have _____ except me. What
                3   4

can I do?

Answer: Moving to a new _____ can be lonely. However, you can
                                            5

make new friends easily. Here's my advice: Even though it's summer, visit your college.

_____ often take _____ in the summer, so there are
                6   7

many _____ on campus, even in summer. Join a club, hang out at the
                8

Student Union, or get a campus job.

Chapter 1: Personality and Learning
Part 2 Social Language

A. Listening for the Main Idea (page 9)

B. Listening for Details (page 9)

Kevin: Hi. My name's Kevin with Campus TV. May I ask you a question about anxiety, stress? Do you do something to reduce stress?

Person 1: Well, yes. I do yoga about three times a week.

Kevin: Great. O.K. Thanks. Excuse me. Can I ask you a question for Campus TV? What do you do about stress?

Person 2: Um, well, I go hiking whenever I can. You know. In the mountains. Fresh air. Sunshine. Nature.

Kevin: Well, thank you. Can I ask you about stress?

Person 3: Uh, I try to meditate once a day. But, um, it's hard to find time.

Kevin: How 'bout you?

Person 4: Running. Every day for an hour.

Kevin: Wow. Rain or shine?

Person 4: Uh-huh. Rain or shine.

Kevin: Cool, thanks. What do you do to relax?

Person 5: Um, gardening. I work in the garden.

Kevin: Thanks. What helps you unwind?

Person 6: Well, I do Tai Chi in the park. Like this … [does Tai Chi pose]

Kevin: Interesting. Very interesting. Hi there! How do you relax?

Person 7: You kidding? Relaxing? What's that? I don't have time for that. Sorry.

Kevin: What helps you reduce stress?

Person 8: Oh, I don't know. I guess I do deep breathing. Not really regularly, but if there's a big problem at work or something I usually try to take a few deep breaths [breathes deeply]. But then I usually blow up [throws hands up in the air], anyway.

Kevin: So, I guess it doesn't work, huh?

Person 8: No, I guess not.

Kevin: Well, thanks for your time.

Part 3 The Mechanics of Listening and Speaking

C. Reduced Forms of Words (page 12)

1. **A:** Whatcher name?

   B: Sarah.

   A: Howdaya spell that?

   B: S-A-R-A-H.

   A: Cudja repeat that?

2. **A:** 'Scuse me. May I ask you something?

   B: I dunno. It depends.

   A: Whadaya do about stress?

   B: I try to exercise every day.

Part 4 Broadcast English

A. Listening for Main Ideas (page 16)

B. Listening for Details (page 16)

Joel: This is Joel Baxter with *Morning News Extra*. Our guest today is Dr. Anna Gardner, a consultant with the State Department of Education. Dr. Gardner's latest book is on how stress affects learning. I'd like to welcome Dr. Gardner to the program.

Dr. Gardner: It's a pleasure to be here, Joel. Thank you for inviting me.

Joel: First of all, could you explain what stress is and why it has an effect on learning?

Dr. Gardner: Sure. Stress is your body's reaction

to something difficult. When we feel stress, our hearts beat faster, our hands may sweat, and sometimes we get anxious. People respond to stress in different ways. Sometimes, a little stress makes us do better. For example, when students have a test, they feel a little extra pressure and so often study more. For most people, too much stress makes learning more difficult. When students are really worried, or have way too much to do, their brains can't really take in new information. All that worry just crowds everything else out.

Joel: How can you tell if a student has too much stress?

Dr. Gardner: Well, one sign that students are not handling stress well is when they avoid assignments. If someone isn't studying for tests or is putting off major projects, he or she is not coping very well with the stress.

Joel: What advice can you give students?

Dr. Gardner: Students should learn to study better. They need to ask questions when something isn't clear. Um, they need to be really well organized.

Joel: Good tip. Anything else?

Dr. Gardner: They should use their time more wisely, and above all, learn to relax.

Part 5 Academic English

A. Listening for Main Ideas (page 20)

Cassie: Hi. I'm Cassie Lee, and I'll be your guide on this tour of City College. Welcome! I'll show you around, and then I'll tell you a little about one of my favorite places.

Here you see a map of City College. Please follow along with me. Right now we're at the entrance to the college. It's on the south side of the campus. Go north on College Way just a little. On your left, you see the Student Services Center. This is a good place to start. This is where new students get information about the college.

Across from the Student Services Center is the Learning Resources Center. Then, next to the Learning Resources Center is the library. It's a beautiful new building. Across from the Library, on your left, you see the bookstore. The snack bar is next to the bookstore. It's between the bookstore and theater arts.

Now, if you continue north, you'll come to the corner of College Way and Valley Walk. On your right is the art center. I love that place! Next to that is a little coffee shop. Then, on your right, is the social science building. Classes in psychology, anthropology, sociology, and political science are here in the social science building.

Now let's go left, or west, a little. Across College Way, on your left, is the physical science building. Here, there are classes in chemistry, geology, and engineering. The music building is between physical science and the humanities building. Do you see it? Students give wonderful concerts in the music building every month. In the humanities building, there are classes in languages, history, and film.

Across from humanities, on Valley Walk, is the Automotive Technology Center. Here, students learn to repair cars. Next to automotive technology is the life science building. Here, in life science, there are classes in subjects like biology and food science.

Let's move up College Way to the north side of campus. Here is the P.E. building. Do you see it over there in the corner? Of course, the gym is here, in the P.E. building. And you see the tennis court and track. And there, next to the P.E. building, is a wonderful place—the college garden. It's a quiet place to sit and study—or meditate! Spring is the best season in the garden. It's full of flowers then.

So that's our campus. I hope you can come and visit it in person.

B. Listening for Details (page 21)

Cassie: Now, if you continue north, you'll come to the corner of College Way and Valley Walk. On your right is the art center. I love that place! Next to that is a little coffee shop. Then, on your right, is the social science building. Classes in psychology, anthropology, sociology, and political science are here in the social science building.

Now let's go left, or west, a little. Across College Way, on your left, is the physical science building. Here, there are classes in chemistry, geology, and engineering. The music building is between physical science and The humanities building. Do you see it? Students give wonderful concerts in the music building every month. In the humanities building, there are classes in languages, history, and film.

Across from humanities, on Valley Walk, is the Automotive Technology Center. Here, students learn to repair cars. Next to automotive technology is the life science building. Here, in life science, there are classes in subjects like biology and food science.

C. Listening to a Personal Story (page 21)

Cassie: Now let me tell you about one place that can really help you.

It's the Student Services Center. In this building, students can get help with academic counseling—you know, help choosing classes, choosing a major, understanding what possible careers there are after graduation. This is what helped me a lot because I didn't know what to major in. I was so confused. I was interested in psychology, but I *loved* music. Also, I was under a lot of stress because my parents didn't want me to be a musician. Well, I went to an academic counselor, and he showed me how to put music and psychology *together*. Before I went to the academic counselor, I didn't know it, but there is a career in music therapy. Now I'm happy, and my parents are, too.

Chapter 2: Learning and Memory Part 2 Social Language

A. Listening for Main Ideas (page 30)

B. Listening for Details (page 31)

Rachel: Hey Ashley.

Ashley: Hi Rachel. What's up?

Rachel: Oh not much, except I've got this big biology midterm, and I'm really worried about it.

Ashley: Why?

Rachel: I don't know... there's so much to learn!

I don't know what to do. There's so much vocabulary to remember!

Ashley: Oh, yeah. I know what you're talking about ... the "Biology of the Human Body" midterm. Yeah, there's a lot to memorize for that.

Rachel: How did you do it? You must have a super memory.

Ashley: Not really, But when I took that class, I got a *big* stack of 3 by 5 cards and wrote all the terms on them. I carried them everywhere I went, and I tested myself all the time.

Rachel: I did that! The problem is *remembering* them all.

Ashley: Oh, O.K. Um ... well, are you using mnemonics?

Rachel: Mnem-*what*-ics?

Ashley: Mnemonics: memory tricks, like "I before E except after C"

Rachel: Oh, yeah ... like rhymes.

Ashley: Yeah, rhymes. Acronyms are another mnemonic, like "Roy G. Biv," *R* for red, *O* for orange, *Y* for yellow, *G* for green, *B* for blue, *I* for indigo, *V* for violet, for the colors of the rainbow.

Rachel: Yeah. That sounds good, but for a big list of biology terms...

Ashley: O.K. Here's a good one: It's called "the method-of-place technique."

Rachel: Method-of-place...

Ashley: Yeah. It's perfect for body parts, especially bones.

Rachel: O.K. How does it work?

Ashley: You memorize a setting or place in detail, like the street you live on. You make a ...uh, a mental map of it.

Rachel: O.K. ...

Ashley: Yeah. Then you remember a certain order in which you visit each place on the map.

Rachel: O.K., like I imagine going north from the bus stop up Oak Street, uh, to my apartment?

Ashley: Right. Then put the things you want to remember in that same order. Like the foot is the bus stop and your apartment is the head.

Rachel: O.K. I got it: "I start at the metatarsals; now I'm passing the tarsals. Here comes the fibula …"

Ashley: You got it!

Rachel: Thanks!

Ashley: All right, well I'll see you later.

Rachel: O.K. Have a good class.

Ashley: Good luck.

Rachel: Thanks.

Part 3 The Mechanics of Listening and Speaking

A. Wh- Questions (page 33)

1. Is there a lot to memorize?
2. How did you do that?
3. What memory trick did you use?
4. Does it work?
5. How does it work?
6. What's your learning style?
7. Are you a visual learner?
8. When do you take the midterm?

C. Asking How to Do Something (page 34)

1. I've got a memory trick. It's good for the colors of the rainbow.
2. Here's a song. It's perfect for remembering the days of the week.
3. I memorized 100 terms for my biology midterm!
4. I know a memory trick. It's called "method of place."
5. I know how to remember people's names.
6. In my language, we have a rhyme. it's great for memorizing the months of the year.

Part 4 Broadcast English

A. Listening for the Main Idea (page 38)

B. Listening for Details (page 38)

Nora: Welcome to Weekend Spotlight. I'm Nora Blake. Today my guest is Lydia Park, student advisor at Midtown Community College. She's here to talk about how recent research can help us understand the issues affecting 18- to 24-year-old students better. Welcome to the program.

Lydia: Thanks for having me on the show.

Nora: First, Lydia, can you tell us about the new research findings?

Lydia: Sure. Well, um, scientists know that we have most of our brain cells before we are even born. Our brains also remove, or *prune*, the brain cells they don't need before we are born. We've learned recently that the teenage brain goes through another period of growth and pruning. The new finding is that the human brain is not really mature until we are in our early to mid-twenties.

Nora: This is really interesting. So what does that mean in terms of the college student?

Lydia: Every parent knows that teenagers think differently. We now believe that the part of the brain that controls decision-making is the last to mature.

Nora *(laughs lightly)*: Some college students might not be very happy to hear that!

Lydia *(chuckles)*: No, I guess not.

Nora: O.K., so 18- to 24-year-olds may have trouble with decision-making. How does that affect them as students?

Lydia: Well, for one thing, it's hard for them to make the decision to study if there's something more fun to do. So, we offer classes that help with decision-making and time management. This helps them become better students.

Nora: Are there other differences in the brains of these young people that affect them as students?

Lydia: Great question. It seems like young people may have differences in the ways their memories work, too. You can imagine that memory is crucial to students.

Nora: How do you help with that?

Lydia: Well, we teach them how to read *actively*, such as making charts with information from their reading. And also getting together with other students—you know, in a small study group—to *talk* about the material they're studying.

Nora: To review it.

Lydia: Right. Reviewing what they have learned within 24 hours is the best way.

C. Guessing the Meaning from Context
(page 39)

1. **Lydia:** Sure. Well, um, scientists know that we have most of our brain cells before we are even born. Our brains also remove or *prune*, the brain cells they don't need before we are born. We've learned recently that the teenage brain goes through another period of growth and pruning. The new finding is that the human brain is not really mature until we are in our early to mid-twenties.

2. **Lydia:** Well, we teach them how to *read actively*, such as making charts with information from their reading. And also getting together with other students—you know, in a small study group—to *talk* about the material they're studying.

Part 5 Academic English

A. Listening for Main Ideas (page 41)

B. Listening for Details (page 42)

Presenter: Hi. Welcome. Welcome to the City College Learning Center. And welcome to our series on "Becoming a Super Student." Today's presentation is "An Introduction to Learning Styles".

First of all, what's a learning style? And what is your learning style? Well, your learning style is basically the way that you learn best. There are many ways to learn, to acquire new information. For example, by reading, by listening, and by doing [counts off the three ways on her fingers]. And although most of us get information by combining these ways, many people prefer to get information by *one* of these ways. That is, they enjoy it more or it's easier to learn for them [points to the word *dominant* on the board]. This is their *dominant* learning

style—the one they use the most.

Learning specialists often talk about three types of learners: [points to *Visual* on the board] Visual—that's learning by seeing. [points to *Auditory* on the board] Auditory—that's learning by listening. And [points to *Kinesthetic* on the board] kinesthetic—that means learning by doing. *Kinesthetic* comes from the Greek word for "movement."

So how do you find out which type you are? Well, we have some ways to help you figure that out right here at the Learning Resources Center. There are short quizzes that are really quite fun to take, and they can give you an idea. And we've got a quick one for you to take at the end of this presentation. Some of you may already have an idea—for example, you might find reading difficult, but you enjoy lectures. So, you might be more of an auditory learner [points to *Auditory* on the board].

Section 2

So why do you need to know your learning style? Well, if you know your learning style, you can make it work even better for you by using learning strategies that match that style.

For example, as you know, you have to do a lot of reading in college. So, if you're a visual learner, [points to *Visual*] you might try seeing pictures in your head as you read. If you're an auditory learner, [points to *Auditory*] you might try reading the material into a tape recorder and listening to it later. [points to *Kinesthetic*] Kinesthetic learners do really well in study groups. So, if you're kinesthetic, you might wanna try reciting and summarizing your material for your study group.

Section 3

One thing I want point out, though, is that you shouldn't think that just because one learning style is dominant for you that you can't improve your ability to learn with another style. For example, let's say you're primarily an auditory learner. That doesn't mean you can't become a better visual learner. Auditory learners sometimes have trouble with reading. But you can become a better reader. In fact, we have a lot of information right here in the Learning

Resources Center on how to become a better reader.

In addition, studies show that many people *retain* new information *better*—in other words, they remember it longer—if they get information in more than one way. So combining learning styles [gestures at the whole list of learning styles] can make you an even *better* learner. For example, you can listen to taped material and read it at the same time. That's auditory plus visual [points to *Auditory* and *Visual*]. Or you can draw graphic organizers while you listen. That's kinesthetic plus auditory [points to *Kinesthetic* and *Auditory*]. See what I mean? O.K.

O.K. Are there any questions? Well if not, let's take the quiz. Um, does anyone need a pencil? O.K.

C. Guessing the Meaning from Context
(page 44)

1. And although most of us get information by combining these ways, many people prefer to get information by one of these ways. That is, they enjoy it more or it's easier to learn for them. This is their *dominant* learning style—the one they use the most [points to *Dominant* on the board].

2. In addition, studies show that many people *retain* new information better—in other words, they remember it longer—if they get information in more than one way.

Chapter 3: Career Choices
Part 2 Social Language

A. Listening for Main Ideas (page 57)

B. Listening for Details (page 57)

Rachel: Can we take a break?

Ashley: Yeah, let's.

Mike: Good idea.

Ashley: Some more coffee? How 'bout some cake?

Rachel: No more coffee for me, thanks.

Mike: Me neither. But cake sounds good.

Rachel: Yeah! Is this that fabulous homemade cake of yours?

Ashley: Uh-huh. I made it this morning.

Mike: Great!

Rachel: Ashley, are these books yours? *What Should I Do with My Life? Choosing Your Career.*

Mike: No, mine. I went to see the college counselor today.

Rachel: How come?

Mike: I'm trying to figure out what to major in.

Rachel: I thought your major was business.

Mike: Um, well, I guess it is.

Ashley: You guess?

Mike: Well, I don't like it a lot. Business was my father's idea.

Rachel: Oh, he wants you to study something practical, huh?

Ashley: Something with a good job after college, hmm?

Mike: Yeah.

Rachel: So what do you want to do with your life?

Mike: Music. I wanna be a rock musician.

Ashley: Cool! I didn't know that.

Rachel: But not very practical, huh?

Mike: Right. That's the problem.

Rachel: Yeah. You never know if you can support yourself …

Ashley: … find a job …

Mike: … pay the bills. So what do I do?

Ashley: Well, maybe there *is* something.

Mike: Yeah?

Ashley: How 'bout the music *business*? There's a really cool college—

Rachel: —the one in Boston?

Ashley: Uh-huh, where you study some instrument—

Mike: —like guitar?

Ashley: Yeah. But you *also* study the music *business*.

Rachel: So you can do what you love—

Ashley: —guitar—

Rachel: —and something practical. You can do *both*.

Mike: Cool! I'll check it out. How much do I owe you? For the advice.

Ashley: Oh, it's free this time. But you guys can give *me* some advice. What can I major in?

Rachel: Cooking!

Mike: Baking!

Rachel: The restaurant business!

Mike: You'll be rich! This cake is amazing.

Ashley: Well, thanks. But somehow, I don't think that's gonna happen.

C. Making Inferences from the Sound of Someone's Voice (page 58)

1. **Mike:** No, mine. I went to see the college counselor today.

    Rachel: How come?

    Mike: I'm trying to figure out what to major in.

2. **Rachel:** So what do you want to do with your life?

    Mike: Music. I want to be a rock musician.

3. **Rachel:** So you can do what you love—

    Ashley: —guitar—

    Rachel: —*and* something practical. You can do *both*.

    Mike: Cool! I'll check it out.

Part 3 The Mechanics of Listening and Speaking

D. Reduced Forms of Words (page 62)

1. **A:** Hi, Emma. What's wrong?

    B: I lost my book. What am I gonna do?

2. **A:** Hey Emma, what's your major?

    B: I'm tryna figure that out.

3. **A:** I enjoy cooking and business. What should I study?

    B: How 'bout the restaurant business?

4. **A:** What's the answer to the first problem?

    B: I'm tryna figure it out.

5. **A:** I'd like to combine music *and* business.

    B: Well, how 'bout majoring in the music business?

G. Hearing the difference between /θ/ and /s/ (page 64)

1. thing	**4.** path
2. tense	**5.** sick
3. think	**6.** sank

Part 4 Broadcast English

A. Listening for the Main Idea (page 67)

C. Listening for General Information (page 68)

D. Listening for Specific Information (page 69)

Tyler: Good morning. This is Business Life, and I'm your host Tyler Donovan. Are you thinking about a career in business? Maybe you're just starting out, or maybe you want to make a career change. Most employees don't stay with the same job or even at the same company for their entire career. With job change almost certain, how do you find out what career is right for you? Today I'm talking with a panel of three young people who are just starting in the business world. You'll hear from Ben Lee, who works in a coffee bar, Miriam Nasser, who's working on a horse farm, and Luke Grandin, who's just started with a software company. Welcome to the program.

Ben: It's nice to be here.

Miriam: Thank you.

Luke: Thanks a lot.

Tyler: Ben, tell me about your job in a coffee bar. It sounds more like a temporary job than a career.

Ben: I know. My parents are a little worried I'll be serving coffee for life.

Tyler: Yeah. It's not really the career I'd pick for a college graduate.

Ben: But I see it as a stepping-stone. Right now, I'm, uh, behind the bar, but they have a great management-training program. See, I want to become a manager and then, well, I want to start my own coffee bar and music place.

Tyler: So you're getting some on the job experience, huh? O.K., Miriam, how'd you come to work on a horse farm and what do you do?

Miriam: Actually, it's not just a farm. It's one of the best-known facilities that, um, trains racehorses. Right now, I'm a hot-walker. That means I just, um, walk the horses around. But as part of my internship, I get to help the trainer.

Tyler: Is that what you want to do?

Miriam: Yeah. I want to open my own training facility. This way I get to learn about everything that happens on a big farm. I love it.

Tyler: All right, Luke. Tell us how you got your job.

Luke: Well, I've always liked computer stuff, and I thought it'd be really cool to get a job working with computers. But, uh, I wasn't really doing so great in school. So, uh, this counselor at school set me up with a job-shadowing thing.

Tyler: Can you explain what that is?

Luke: Yeah. I basically just followed this guy around at work. He does computer graphics. Well, it was some interesting stuff, so I decided to study that at school. I got my degree and well…

Tyler: Now you work there yourself?

Luke: Yeah, pretty cool, huh?

Tyler: So it sounds like, from the experiences of our three guests today, that you can explore different careers through a variety of ways: training programs on the job, internships, and job-shadowing.

B. Guessing the Meaning from Context
(page 67)

1. **Miriam:** Actually, it's not just a farm. It's one of the best-known facilities that, um, trains racehorses. Right now, I'm a hot-walker. That means I just, um, walk the horses around. But as part of my internship, I get to help the trainer.

2. **Luke:** So, uh, this counselor at school set me

up with a job-shadowing thing.

Tyler: Can you explain what that is?

Luke: Yeah. I basically just followed this guy around at work. He does computer graphics.

Part 5 Academic English

A. Listening for Main Ideas (page 72)

Presenter: Good afternoon, and welcome to the Career Center. This is "An Introduction to the City College Career Center," and my name is David Martinez. Today's presentation is in two parts. In the first part, I'm gonna describe the services we have here at the center. Then I'm gonna talk about things that you can do, uh, *while* you're a student to prepare for your career *after* you graduate.

B. Listening for Details (page 72)

C. Listening for Examples (page 72)

Presenter: O.K. Let's get started. First of all, if you want to work during the school year, this is the place to come. We have job listings of all types here. You can find a part-time job or a full-time, summer job. You can find an, uh, an on-campus job or an off-campus job. You can also get information on internships, volunteer jobs, and jo-, uh, job-shadowing opportunities. Does everyone know what job-shadowing is? Great.

O.K. We also organize events. The Career Center has two career fairs every school year. At a career fair, representatives from companies and other organizations come to campus. This is a great way to learn about different organizations and the job opportunities they have.

We also have on-campus interviewing events. This is when um company representatives come to campus and give interviews for job openings.

Career resources are another service we offer. We have workshops on things like writing resumes and interviewing skills. You can, uh, also find answers to the question "What do I do with my major?" We have books, videos, and CD-ROMs with information on different careers.

We also offer career counseling. You can take aptitude tests to figure out, uh, what kinds of, uh, careers might be best for you, and you can meet with counselors who can help you choose a major and a career.

D. Listening for Details (page 72)

Presenter: Now many students—and especially their parents—worry about what they'll be able to do after graduation. Well, there's a lot you can do *while* you're a student to help prepare for your career. Here're some tips:

First of all, uh, come to the Career Center to get help on choosing a major. Find out all you can about the types of occupations that your major might lead to. And make sure that you take courses related to your career choice.

Secondly, if possible, get a part-time job or a summer job doing something related to your career choice. Let me give you an example. One student here was an education major. He wanted to be an elementary school teacher. The whole time he was here, he worked part time in a classroom in an elementary school across town. He got on-the-job experience and got to know everyone at the school and they got to know him. And you know what? They hired him as soon as he finished his studies,

Volunteering or doing an internship is another great way to prepare for a career while you're a student. If you, uh, get a volunteer job or an internship in an organization that you'd like to work for when you graduate, you get valuable experience and also have a good chance of working for that company later on.

Finally, many professors here do consulting work for companies. You want to try and network with professors who have connections in industries or, uh, companies that interest you. Here's an example: a business major I know had a professor who was working on a project for Apple Computer. The professor asked her to help him on the project. She got to know many people at Apple this way. They liked her, and they hired her after she graduated.

O.K. Well, that's about it for now. Any questions?

Chapter 4: Marketing for the Ages
Part 2 Social Language

A. Listening for the Main Idea (page 80)

B. Listening for Details (page 80)

Ashley: So Rachel, tell me about your new job.

Rachel: Sure…

Mike: You got a job, Rachel?

Rachel: Well, it's not a regular job. I'm a trend spotter.

Mike: What's that?

Rachel: I look for youth trends and report on them.

Mike: Like a newspaper reporter?

Rachel: No, I work for a market research company.

Ashley: What do you report on?

Rachel: Well … uh, what people are wearing, what movies they're seeing…

Mike: Really?

Ashley: Just anybody?

Rachel: No. The research company only wants information on youth trends.

Mike: What are "youth trends"?

Rachel: Well, it's mainly what 8- to 24-year-olds are doing.

Ashley: Why is that important?

Rachel: Companies that make or market products need to know what appeals to this age group of 8- to 24- year-olds.

Mike: Why?

Rachel: Because it's an important market. They can make a lot of money if they appeal to that group.

Mike: Uh-huh…

Ashley: So what *exactly* do you do?

Rachel: I notice things. For example, what girls are wearing to school, what kind of cell phones people use…

Ashley: Oh, yeah…

Rachel: Things like the abbreviations that kids use in chat rooms, what TV shows are popular…

Ashley: Uh-huh…

Rachel: So, I email reports on stuff like this to the company about once a month.

Mike: And...and you get paid for this?

Rachel: Yeah! I get about 75 dollars for each report.

Mike: Sounds like easy work ... can I do it?

Rachel: I dunno ... you have to be good at noticing things. You know, they do need people who play a lot of online games.

Mike: Oh!

Ashley: That sounds like you, Mike.

Rachel: All you have to do is answer questions for that job.

Mike: Sounds perfect for me! Where do I sign up?

Part 3 The Mechanics of Listening and Speaking

B. Hearing the Difference Between /I/ and /i/ (page 82)

1. he's	**6.** live
2. each	**7.** seek
3. sit	**8.** a pill
4. lead	**9.** bit
5. it	**10.** teen

E. Understanding Interjections (page 83)

1. **A:** Do you have the course syllabus?
   B: Uh-uh. [meaning "no"]

2. **A:** Do you like your new job?
   B: Uh-huh. [meaning "yes"]

3. **A:** We have an exam today.
   B: Uh-oh. [meaning "problem" or "trouble"]

4. **A:** Young people buy a lot of stuff, so companies are trying to appeal to them.
   B: Uh-huh! [meaning "Oh, now I understand."]

5. **A:** Do you like that TV show?
   B: Uh ... [meaning "I'm not sure what to say."]

Part 4 Broadcast English

A. Listening for the Main Idea (page 89)

B. Listening for Details (page 90)

Jack: Good evening. I'm Jack Hammond and this is Shoptalk. Tonight we're going to talk about what's cool, what's hot, and what's not. Businesses are interested in what cool people are doing, wearing, and playing, and these businesses will pay good money to find it out. My guest is Tina Lane. Tina is a trend-watcher. Tina's company works with a thousand young people ages 10 to 25 to find out what's cool. Welcome to the program, Tina.

Tina: Thank you, Jack. I'm happy to be here.

Jack: Tina, tell us, what exactly does your company do?

Tina: Basically, we collect information on trends and then sell that information to businesses.

Jack: What kind of businesses?

Tina: Mostly two kinds of businesses: um, first, companies that manufacture products. And second, we sell information to advertisers.

Jack: Advertising companies?

Tina: Oh, yeah. They write all those ads for magazines and TV, and you know—

Jack: —those ads are expensive, right?

Tina: Exactly. So advertisers need to figure out how to appeal to kids, especially.

Jack: Why kids?

Tina: Well, uh, kids, young people, actually, are really the trend setters. Most trends *start* with young people. That's why we hire kids from all kinds of places—we find them in malls, cool clothing stores, high schools, and music places. Kids know what's cool.

Jack: So do you just ask them what's cool?

Tina: Um, yes and no. We talk to kids a lot, we interview them, we go to places where kids hang out and just watch them. But that's not the end of it. We take all the information and put it in a database. We look for trends and see what pops out at us from all that data.

Jack: How scientific is this process?

Tina: You know, Jack, it's really a mix of science

and intuition. We can tell a lot from the information, but we also listen to certain people who just seem to be cooler than everyone else. They can spot a trend right away.

Jack: What trends do you see these days?

Tina: Well, as you can guess, new technology is always important. Kids these days are hooked into iPods, laptops, uh … cell phones. For businesses, technology is important because it helps *spread* cool trends. As soon as something becomes cool, kids send it by instant messages to other kids everywhere. Kids become kind of, um, *advertisers* …

C. Listening for Reasons (page 91)

Tina: Kids these days are hooked into iPods, laptops, uh … cell phones. For businesses, technology is important because it helps *spread* cool trends. As soon as something becomes cool, kids send it by instant messages to other kids everywhere. Kids become kind of, um, *advertisers* …

Part 5 Academic English

A. Listening for the Topic (page 94)

Lecturer: Hello.

Class: Hi.

Lecturer: How's everybody? Alright, well, today we're gonna explore something very practical and something you're probably interested in—your own finances—in other words, your own money, *now*, during your years in college, before you go off and begin your career. Maybe some of you already have a few problems with your finances—

Student: Yeah, like not enough money.

Lecturer: Yeah. Yeah, that's often a problem. However, our topic today is not how to *make* money but how to *handle* money that you have. Students in their first year of college often make choices about money that are … well …

Student: Terrible?

Lecturer: Yes. Terrible. I was thinking of, uh, "not very mature," but yes, indeed, sometimes they make decisions that are really,

really bad. This can lead to anxiety and even *more* problems. So today we're going to explore how you can make smart decisions about your own finances in two main areas: credit and advertising.

B. Listening for Details (page 94)

Lecturer: First, credit. Here, in the United States, what percent of students do you think take out a student loan to get through college? In other words, how many students borrow money for books, tuition, so on?

Students: Twenty percent? Thirty percent?

Lecturer: Well, actually, 60 percent [writes *Student Loans—60%* on the board]. That means more than half of all college students borrow money to get through school. Is this a bad thing?

No. Actually, it's not bad. Student loans have very low interest rates [writes *Interest Rates—Low*]. Now student loans have very low interest rates. And students don't have to begin to pay them back until one year after they graduate, when they have a good job. It's not a bad idea to borrow money for your education.

C. Listening for Details (page 95)

Lecturer: The *problem* … is *this* [takes out a credit card and shows it to the class]. Credit cards can get students into big trouble. [draws a T-chart with the headings *Dos* and *Don'ts*] And I'd like to keep you guys outta trouble, so here are some "do's" and "don'ts" for using credit cards. Remember that credit is a *loan*, not free money. You've gotta pay it back.

First, get only *one* credit card [shows the credit card again]—one with a low interest rate. You need to shop around—in other words, check out many different credit cards to find one with a low rate. However, don't get one, let me repeat that. Do *not* get one with a low *introductory* rate; in other words, many credit card companies offer low interest rates just for the first few months only—introductory rates—but then the rates go, wooo, *way* up. Stay away from these [in the *Dos* column, writes *1 credit card, shop around,* and *low interest*] … and the don'ts … don't get low introductory rates [in the *Don'ts* column, writes *don't get low introductory rates*]. Stay away from these. Next, and these are two of my favorites, you want to pay off the balance every month [writes *pay off the balance* under *Dos*], and don't just pay the interest [writes *pay just the interest* under *Don'ts*]. I'll say that again: pay off the balance, and don't pay *just* the interest. If you pay only the interest, you will be in debt for a long, long time. Do not—repeat, do *not*—use one credit card to pay off another. Never use one credit card to pay another card. But of course, if you *have* only one card, this isn't a problem. O.K. Questions?

D. Listening for Details (page 96)

Lecturer: O.K., next week we're gonna study advertising and the *psychology* of advertising. What is the effect of advertising on *you*? How do companies use advertising to make you spend your money? I'll tell you what they *don't* do. These days, most companies do not put real information in their ads. Right? Take a look at ads in magazines or on TV. Almost no information about the product. So what do they do instead? They play with our brains [points to his forehead] to make us want something we do not *need*. Advertisers appeal to young people, especially, right?

I want you to start thinking about the psychology of advertising [draws a T-chart with the headings *Values* and *Ads*]. Think about this. There are values that are important in almost every culture. But advertising appeals to our desire to go *against* our values. For example, greed is not good, [writes *Greed—Bad* under *Values*] greed bad, right? But what does advertising tell us? Greed is *good*. It's important to have really expensive things. That's what advertising tells us, have really expensive things [writes *have really expensive things* under *Ads*]. Another value is that *goodness* is more important than *physical* beauty, goodness [writes *Goodness* under *Values*]. But what ads tell us is that physical attractiveness is what's important [writes *physical attractiveness* under *Ads*]. Physical attractiveness.

Here's what I want you to do for homework: Find five ads on TV or in magazines that are examples of this. Be prepared to discuss them. What are your cultural values? But what

do the *ads* say is important? O.K.? Got it? All right, good. See you Monday.

Chapter 5: Connecting with Others
Part 2 Social Language

A. Listening for Main Ideas (page 108)

B. Listening for Details (page 109)

C. Listening for Opinions (page 109)

Ashley: Hi.

Mike: Hey Ashley!

Ashley: Hi Mike, hey Rachel, what's up?

Rachel: Hey!

Ashley: Are you going to the freshman barbecue tonight?

Rachel: Sure!

Mike: Yeah, maybe …

Rachel: Why "maybe"? Aren't you sure?

Mike: I dunno. All those people … I won't know anyone …

Ashley: But that's the idea!

Rachel: Yeah. You go to these things to meet new people. Don't you want to make some new friends?

Mike: Sure, but I don't think a barbecue is the best way.

Ashley: Why not?

Mike: Because it's just hard to meet someone in a big group.

Rachel: I love meeting people at parties and in big groups!

Ashley: Why?

Rachel: Because you have a lot of choice …there are a lot of people, a lot of possibilities for meeting people.

Mike: But don't you think it's hard to get to know people? Isn't it hard to decide if you really like them?

Ashley: Well, I agree with Mike. It's noisy, there's a lot going on … You can't always have a great conversation.

Mike: That's exactly what I mean.

Rachel: So how *do* you like to meet people, Mike?

Mike: I think small groups are the best way to meet people. I meet the most interesting people in class, both guys and girls. I see how they think and talk every day. Like my psych class. We have a study group. If I like someone in the group, then we might get together later on.

Rachel: You're such a serious guy, Mike! How about you, Ashley?

Ashley: Well, y'know, I met Viktor in the biology club. We knew we had a lot in common. We both like biology. If you ask me, campus clubs are the best way to meet people.

Rachel: Well, maybe … but I'll take my chances at the barbecue. I'll see you guys later!

Part 3 The Mechanics of Listening and Speaking

A. *Reduced Forms of Words with /t/ and /y/* (page 111)

1. Doncha want to meet some new people?
2. Why arenchu going to the barbecue?
3. I like the new English teacher. How 'boutchu?
4. Ashley, I wanchu to meet someone. This is Viktor.
5. The party was fun. Why dinchu go?

C. *Giving an Opinion* (page 112)

1. I think that campus clubs are the best way to meet people.
2. If you ask me, it's hard to get to know people around here.
3. I don't think small groups are the best way to meet people.
4. If you ask me, campus clubs are really fun.
5. I think that you are going to meet some very interesting people in your computer class.
6. I don't think that you should go to a movie on a first date.

D. *Asking for an Opinion* (page 112)

1. I like big parties. How about you?
2. I don't like big groups. What about you?
3. Campus clubs are a good way to meet people. Don't you think?
4. Don't you think a barbecue is the best way to get to know someone?
5. I don't like big parties. What about you?
6. Study groups are a good way to meet interesting people. What do you think?

Part 4 Broadcast English

A. *Listening for Main Ideas* (page 116)

B. *Listening for Details* (page 116)

Host: In 1993, 10-year-old Lydia Compton from McLean, Virginia, heard about a teenager in Poland, Alexi Wasowski, who was a wonderful chess player. Lydia also liked to play chess. She wrote to Alexi, and he wrote back. They wrote to each other for several years, and then they lost touch. Last week the pen pals reunited again for the first time in 12 years. Lydia, tell us about that first letter.

Lydia: Well, I read an article about Alexi when I was in fourth grade and wrote to the chess organization in Poland. They forwarded the letter to Alexi, and to my surprise, he wrote back.

Alexi: Yes. I was very happy to get a letter from the United States. I was learning English in school at that time. Writing to Lydia was a good way to practice my English.

Host: What did you say to each other in those letters?

Lydia: At first, it was a lot about chess.

Alexi: Yes, but well, then, we told each other about our countries, music, movies. Lydia sometimes corrected my English.

Lydia: Not really. Alexi's English was great. But he didn't always understand American slang.

Host: How did you lose touch?

Alexi: When I was 15, my family moved, and I lost her address.

Lydia: Yeah, and the next time I wrote to Alexi, my letter was returned.

Host: After all these years, how did you get back in touch with each other?

Lydia: The wonders of the Internet. I was thinking about Alexi one day and I did a search on his name. I found out he was a graduate student in mathematics here in the United States.

Alexi: Somehow she found my email address. We set up a meeting, and well, here we are. It was amazing to discover that we only lived 30 minutes apart.

Host: Do you think you'll stay in touch this time?

Alexi: For sure. We have a date to play chess next week.

Lydia: Definitely. Now that Alexi and I are getting to know each other again, I think I may get back into chess.

C. Guessing the Meaning from Context
(page 117)

1. **Host:** After all these years, how did you get back in touch with each other?

   Lydia: The wonders of the Internet. I was thinking about Alexi one day and I did a search on his name. I found out he was a graduate student in mathematics here in the United States.

2. **Host:** Do you think you'll *stay in touch* this time?

   Alexi: For sure. We have a date to play chess next week.

Part 5 Academic English

A. Listening for the Main Idea (page 119)

B. Listening For Details (page 120)

C. Checking Your Notes (page 121)

Danielle: Uh...hi, everyone. Thanks for coming. My name is Danielle, and I'm, uh, a junior and uh, I'm majoring in sociology. I'm the moderator today, and I'm gonna introduce you to some of the, uh, campus clubs.

O.K. Campus clubs are organizations that students run. They give students lots of opportunities to learn and do things outside of their academic work.

Uh, there are 32 student-run organizations here on campus. There's a lot of variety. There are academic clubs, service clubs, professional clubs …

And there are a lot of great reasons to join a campus club. First of all, uh, there are opportunities to do volunteer work. You can also get work experience and leadership experience. This leads to success in school and in life. And it looks great on your resume!

In fact, studies show some really interesting things about students and, um, campus clubs. Students who belong to clubs are more involved in school. They're less likely to wanna drop out or transfer if they, um, belong to a club. And students in clubs get better grades than students who don't belong to clubs.

But, uh, really, one of the *best* things about joining a campus club is meeting new people.

O.K. Now, let's hear from some club representatives on the panel today. They're each gonna tell you a little bit about their groups. Um, Viktor, do you wanna start?

Viktor: Sure. Hello everyone. I'm Viktor Ivanov. I run the biology club. The biology club is for anyone who is interested in biology. And, uh, of course, you don't have to be a biology major. We read and talk about biology in the news. We go on field trips, and we have guest speakers. We have a lot of fun, and it's a good place to, uh, to meet interesting people.

Danielle: Thanks, Viktor. Now, let's hear from the International Business Club.

Ashley: Hi. My name is Ashley. I'm the president of the, um, IBC, the International Business Club. The purpose of this club is to … to bring people together who are interested international business, business majors, ah, or just anybody who is interested in international issues. We help students get internships at local cor-, uh, companies. It's a good way to get some real-world experience and, uh, of course, to network.

Danielle: Great, Ashley. Thanks. Um, Winston?

Winston: Hi. I'm, uh, Winston Baek. I'm the vice president of the environment club. We talk about environmental problems, um, both around the world and right here in our community. But we don't just talk. We take action. We organize recycling programs and beach clean ups. Um, we also go around to the elementary schools and, uh, talk to kids, uh, about the environment and how they can help, too. So, uh, the environment club is a great way to do something positive and get leadership experience at the same time.

Chapter 6: Sports and Life
Part 2 Social Language

A. Listening for the Main Idea (page 128)

B. Listening for Details (page 128)

Mike: Hi. My name is Mike. I'm doing an interview for Campus TV. Can I ask you a few questions?

Person 1: Sorry. I'm in a hurry.

Mike: O.K...Hey, Ashley!

Person 2: Hey Mike.

Mike: How ya doin?

Person 2: Good thanks.

Mike: Can I use you in my interview?

Person 2: Sure...

Mike: Great. Um, O.K., my first question is do you, do you play any sports?

Person 2: Yeah, I'm on the college basketball team.

Mike: Oh great, great! Um, why do you play basketball?

Ashley: Well ... it's a great game. It's exciting. It's a great workout.

Mike: Do you like to watch it on TV?

Ashley: No, uh, I just like tuh play it.

Mike: O.K. Thanks. Bye.

Mike: Hey.

Person 3: Hey.

Mike: What's up, Rachel?

Mike: What are you doing?

Mike: Not much. Can I use you for my interview?

Person 3: Sure.

Mike: All right, cool. Uh, I'm doing an interview on sports. And, uh, my first question is, uh, do you play any sports?

Person 3: Nope.

Mike: Nothing?

Person 3: Nope.

Mike: Uh, how about, how 'bout watching sports?

Person 3: Definitely. I love Monday Night Football.

Mike: And, and where do you watch it?

Person 3: Usually with some people at a sports bar.

Mike: And why do you like to watch football on TV?

Person 3: It's actually relaxing. I know people get all excited an' yell an' everything, but after a hard day, it's a great way to relax.

Mike: O.K. Well, thank you very much.

Person 3: You're welcome.

Mike: Excuse me, I'm doing an interview on sports for Campus TV. Can I ask you a few questions?

Person 4: Sports? Sure!

Mike: Do you watch or play any sports?

Person 4: You bet. I'm a P.E. major.

Mike: Oh, so what are you involved in?

Person 4: I play baseball, soccer, and basketball.

Mike: Wow.

Person 4: I also coach a kids' soccer team.

Mike: Why do you do that?

Person 4: Uh, I think sports are really important for kids. Not just kids, but everybody.

Mike: Why's that?

Person 4: I think it helps people do better at everything in life: You learn teamwork, how to work well in groups. You get healthy lifestyle habits ... and, uh, you learn leadership skills.

Mike: Well, great, thanks!

Person 4: You're welcome.

Mike: Bye. Uh, excuse me, can I ask you a few questions for Campus TV?

Person 5: What about?

Mike: I'm doing an interview on sports—what people play and what they watch.

Person 5: I'm into extreme sports. I love to watch that stuff on TV.

Mike: What are "extreme sports"?

Person 5: Risky sports, dangerous sports—

Mike: Such as?

Person 5: Skateboarding, snowboarding, surfing.

Mike: O.K. Do you do any extreme sports?

Person 5: No way!

Mike: Why not?

Person 5: Too dangerous, man! I just like to watch.

Mike: O.K., well, uh, thanks very much.

Person 5: O.K., man.

Mike: Uh, hi. You look like you're into sports. Can I ask you a few questions for campus TV?

Person 6: Uh, is it gonna be on TV?

Mike: Sure.

Person 6: No thanks.

Mike: May I ask why?

Person 6: It's illegal to skateboard on campus, man.

Mike: Oh. What do you like about it?

Person 6: The thrills, man.

Mike: What do you mean, like, doing it where you're not supposed to?

Person 6: Exactly, but it's more than that.

Mike: What else?

Person 6: You're outdoors … and it takes a lot of skills.

Mike: Such as?

Person 6: Balance. Judging distance, time, speed.

Mike: Sounds like physics.

Person 6: Yeah, that too.

Mike: O.K., later, man.

Person 6: Later.

C. Listening for Reasons (page 129)

1. **Mike:** Hey, Ashley!

    Person 2: Hey Mike.

    Mike: How ya doin?

    Person 2: Good thanks.

    Mike: Can I use you in my interview?

    Person 2: Sure.

    Mike: Great. Um, O.K., my first question is do you, do you play any sports?

    Person 2: Yeah, I'm on the college basketball team.

    Mike: Oh great, great! Um, why do you play basketball?

    Ashley: Well … it's a great game. It's exciting. It's a great workout.

    Mike: Do you like to watch it on TV?

    Ashley: No, uh, I just like tuh play it.

2. **Mike:** Can I use you for my interview?

    Person 3: Sure.

    Mike: All right, cool. Uh, I'm doing an interview on sports. And, uh, my first question is, uh, do you play any sports?

    Person 3: Nope.

    Mike: Nothing?

    Person 3: Nope.

    Mike: Uh, how about, how 'bout watching sports?

    Person 3: Definitely. I love Monday Night Football.

    Mike: And, and where do you watch it?

    Person 3: Usually with some people at a sports bar.

    Mike: And why do you like to watch football on TV?

    Person 3: It's actually relaxing. I know people get all excited an' yell an' everything, but after a hard day, it's a great way to relax.

    Mike: O.K. Well, thank you very much.

    Person 3: You're welcome.

3. **Mike:** Excuse me, I'm doing an interview on

sports for Campus TV. Can I ask you a few questions?

Person 4: Sports? Sure!

Mike: Do you watch or play any sports?

Person 4: You bet. I'm a P.E. major.

Mike: Oh, so what are you involved in?

Person 4: I play baseball, soccer, and basketball.

Mike: Wow.

Person 4: I also coach a kids' soccer team.

Mike: Why do you do that?

Person 4: Uh, I think sports are really important for kids. Not just kids, but everybody.

Mike: Why's that?

Person 4: I think it helps people do better at everything in life: You learn teamwork, how to work well in groups. You get healthy lifestyle habits … and, uh, you learn leadership skills.

Mike: Well, great, thanks!

Person 4: You're welcome.

4. **Mike:** Uh, hi. You look like you're into sports. Can I ask you a few questions for campus TV?

Person 6: Uh, is it gonna be on TV?

Mike: Sure

Person 6: No thanks.

Mike: May I ask why?

Person 6: It's illegal to skateboard on campus, man.

Mike: Oh. What do you like about it?

Person 6: The thrills, man.

Mike: What do you mean, like, doing it where you're not supposed to?

Person 6: Exactly.

D. *Guessing the Meaning from General Context* (page 129)

1. **Mike:** O.K. Do you do any extreme sports?

Person 5: No way!

Mike: Why not?

Person 5: Too dangerous, man! I just like to watch.

2. **Person 6:** Balance. Judging distance, time, speed.

Mike: Sounds like physics.

Person 6: Yeah, that too.

Mike: O.K., later, man.

Person 6: Later.

3. **Mike:** Do watch or play any sports?

Person 4: You bet. I'm a P.E. major.

Mike: Oh, so what are you involved in?

Part 3 The Mechanics of Listening and Speaking

B. *Reduced Forms of Words* (page 132)

1. I like tuh play tennis and golf.

2. Do you like tuh watch football an' soccer on TV?

3. I'm doin' my homework and then I'm watchin' TV.

4. I like watchin' sports. I'm not intuh playin' sports.

5. I'm intuh skateboardin' an' surfin'.

D. *Hearing the Difference Between /æ/ and /a/* (page 132)

1. hat	6. pat
2. ad	7. sock
3. box	8. cot
4. racket	9. black
5. mop	

Part 4 Broadcast English

A. *Listening for the Main Idea* (page 138)

B. *Listening for Details* (page 138)

Terry: Welcome to Sportstime. I'm Terry Bracken. Most people know about the benefits of sports. People who play sports develop skills, learn to work with a team, and stay in excellent physical health. Also, sports provide entertainment to fans and a sense of community. Fans support their local teams, and this is all good. But lately we are seeing more inappropriate behavior and even violence at sporting events. Today, we're here to talk about inappropriate behavior in sports. My guest is Dr. Howard Green, a psychologist and professor at Melton University. Welcome to the program, Dr. Green.

Dr. Green: Thank you for having me on your program. Great to be here.

Terry: Dr. Green, first of all, just what kind of violent behavior are we talking about?

Dr. Green: Well, we're seeing two definite problem areas. First, there is the violence on the field, you know between players, between coaches and officials, and in some cases among the fans.

Terry: Yes, that's the kind of thing you see on TV, right?

Dr. Green: Exactly. Like when the fan throws a bottle at a player, or when a player tries to shut a fan up. The other problem area is after the game. That's when fans fight or burn cars or break windows.

Terry: Yeah, we've all seen that happen. But why is it that sports seem to, um, encourage violence, and other forms of group entertainment don't?

Dr. Green: Great question. We've got some ideas about that. You know, fans really identify with their teams. They form connections with other fans. You've seen fans who paint their faces in the team's colors or come to games in costumes, it's all good fun.

Terry: Yeah, yeah, like those guys who take off their shirts and paint their chests, even when it's freezing outside?

Dr. Green: Exactly. When the team wins, you win. But, when your team loses, so do you. Other things can contribute to violence— alcohol, the influence of a crowd, poor examples set by professional athletes.

Terry: Wow. It seems like a pretty big problem. Is there any way to solve it?

Dr. Green: Actually, there's quite a few ways. For example, colleges can really discourage the drinking of alcohol at games. They can also stop general rowdy behavior before and during the game.

Terry: What else?

Dr. Green: Uh, well, sports organizations at the college and professional level should really punish players and coaches for poor behavior. That would provide a better example for the fans.

Terry: Do you think we in the media have any responsibility?

Dr. Green: Absolutely. If TV stops showing inappropriate behavior, people won't think it's so acceptable.

Terry: Well, thank you very much for talking with us today.

C. Listening for Causes and Effects (page 139)

Dr. Green: Exactly. When the team wins, you win. But, when your team loses, so do you. Other things can contribute to violence— alcohol, the influence of a crowd, poor examples set by professional athletes.

Terry: Wow. It seems like a pretty big problem. Is there any way to solve it?

D. Listening for Solutions to Problems (page 139)

Terry: Wow. It seems like a pretty big problem. Is there any way to solve it?

Dr. Green: Actually, there's quite a few ways. For example, colleges can really discourage the drinking of alcohol at games. They can also stop general rowdy behavior before and during the game.

Terry: What else?

Dr. Green: Uh, well, sports organizations at the college and professional level should really punish players and coaches for poor behavior. That would provide a better example for the fans.

Terry: Do you think we in the media have any responsibility?

Dr. Green: Absolutely. If TV stops showing inappropriate behavior, people won't think it's so acceptable.

Part 5 Academic English

A. Listening for Main Ideas (page 142)

D. Checking Your Notes (page 145)

Presenter: Well, I hope you all had a nice lunch. O.K., for this part of the orientation, we're going to talk about sports and recreation at City College. Uh, I'm going to give you an overview of the different ways you can participate in sports here, including team opportunities and the things you can do at the Tiger Recreation Center.

First of all, uh, how many of you are planning to try to get on teams here? Good. I see a lot of hands going up. Excellent. How many of you were on teams in high school? Wonderful! O.K. And how many of you just like to get a good workout occasionally? Very good! It looks like we have a group of students with good lifestyle habits.

Well, everyone knows the advantages of regular exercise, especially for students—you're gonna find that occasionally you'll be coping with stress. And a good workout is a great way to reduce stress. And of course, being on a team has advantages. You get teamwork and leadership opportunities that can help you later on in life, such as in your career.

B. Listening for Details (page 143)

D. Checking Your Notes (page 145)

Presenter: Well, let's see what City College offers.

City College has intercollegiate and intramural teams. That's intercollegiate and intramural. Our intercollegiate teams compete with other colleges in the Western Valley Association. The colleges in this association that we compete with include Eastern State, Bay College, Greenhill College, Valley College, and Brandon. I'm sure you've seen some of the games and you know the competition from these teams can be tough, which makes the games exciting.

O.K. Intercollegiate teams in the fall and winter include football, men's soccer, women's soccer, men's basketball, and women's basketball. In the spring, we have baseball, softball, swimming and track and field.

Just to give you a little information on the goals of intercollegiate athletics here at City, we think it's an important part of the whole academic experience. The intercollegiate athletic program provides student-athletes with the opportunity to form connections with each other and provides a sense of community. We think this is a crucial part of campus life. Students identify with the teams and this affects campus life in a positive way.

So, if you are a competitive player with team experience, intercollegiate athletics might be good for you. Students who want to participate in intercollegiate athletics must see an advisor and you need to have a grade point average of 2.0 or higher.

By the way, if you like to watch sports, there's nothing more exciting than watching the City College Tigers. And the players really appreciate our support, so come on out to the games as often as you can. Look for the intercollegiate game schedule on the college calendar.

C. Listening for Details (page 143)

D. Checking Your Notes (page 145)

Presenter: O.K. If you just want to have some fun with team sports, you might want to explore the intramural teams. Intramural teams play against other teams within the college. Intramural sports here at City College are fun and informal. We have a lot of different men's, women's, and coed sports including basketball, volleyball, indoor soccer, swimming, softball, badminton, and tennis. We even have a Frisbee team. You can play on a regular basis if you want or just come by and join a team when you feel like playing.

Participation on intramural teams is free and the college provides all the equipment you need. You must follow the intramural team guidelines and use the correct equipment at all times. This is for your safety.

Teams meet at the Tiger Recreation Center. You can find a list of the teams and activities there and the schedules are also listed on the school website.

VOCABULARY INDEX

SKILLS INDEX

CREDITS

Photo Credits

Cover: top right: © Michael Rosefeld/Getty Images; middle left: © Skip Nall/Getty Images; bottom right: The McGraw-Hill Companies Inc.

Getting Started. p. xii (left): © Getty Images, © BananaStock/PictureQuest, © Digital Vision; p. xii (right): © Michael Rosefeld/Getty Images, © Skip Nall/Getty Images, The McGraw-Hill Companies Inc.; p. xiii: © BananaStock/PictureQuest; p. xiv (top): The McGraw-Hill Companies Inc.; p. xiv (bottom): © Digital Vision/PictureQuest.

Unit 1. Opener: © BananaStock/PictureQuest; p. 3: © BananaStock/PictureQuest; p. 5 (top): © Royalty-Free/CORBIS; p. 5 (bottom): Verve Commissioned Series/Getty Images; p. 7 (left): © Digital Vision; p. 7 (right): © Royalty-Free/CORBIS; p. 15, 18: © Verve Commissioned Series/Getty Images; p. 25: © BananaStock/PictureQuest; p. 26 (all): Linda S. O'Roke; p. 29: The McGraw-Hill Copmanies Inc./Ken Cavanagh Photograher; p. 30 (top): © Robert Glusic/Getty Images; p. 30 (bottom): © BananaStock/PictureQuest; p. 41: David S. Averbach.

Unit 2. Opener: © Brand X Pictures/PicturQuest; p.51: © Brand X Pictures/PicturQuest; p. 52 (top): © Digital Vision/Getty Images; p. 52 (middle and bottom): © Royalty-Free/CORBIS; p. 56, 58 (all), 60: The McGraw-Hill Companies Inc.; p. 65 (left): © Adam Crowley/Getty Images; p. 65 (middle): © Doug Menuez/Getty Images; p. 65 (right): © Michael Rosefeld/Getty Images; p. 66 (left): © Adam Crowley/Getty Images; p. 66 (middle): © Doug Menuez/Getty Images; p. 66 (right): © Michael Rosefeld/Getty Images; p. 75: © Jack Hollingsworth/Getty Images; p. 76 (top): The McGraw-Hill Companies Inc.; p. 76 (bottom): © PhotoDisc/Getty Images; p. 80: The McGraw-Hill Companies Inc.; p. 88: © Tony Anderson/Getty Images; p. 92: © Digital Vision/PictureQuest.

Unit 3. Opener: © Skip Nall/Getty Images; p. 103: © BananaStock/PictureQuest; p. 104: © Digital Vision/Getty Images; p. 105 (top): © C. Borland/PhotoLink/Getty Images; p. 105 (bottom): © Buccina Studios/Getty Images; p. 107 (top left): © image 100/Getty Images; p. 107 (top right): © BananaStock/PictureQuest; p. 107 (bottom): © Digital Vision/Getty Images; p. 108: The McGraw-Hill Companies Inc.; p. 116 (both): © Digital Vision/Getty Images; p. 119 David S. Averbach; p. 123 © Ryan McVay/Getty Images; p. 124 (top left and top middle): © Royalty-Free/CORBIS; p. 124 (top right): © Ryan McVay/Getty Images; p. 124 (bottom left): © McGraw-Hill Companies, Inc./Gary He, photographer; p. 124 (bottom middle): © Lawrence M. Sawyer/Getty Images; p. 124 (bottom right): © Steve Cole/Getty Images; p. 127 (top left): © Image Source/ PictureQuest; p. 127 (right): © Karl Weatherly/Getty Images; p. 127 (bottom left): © Royalty-Free/CORBIS; p. 136: © Owen Franken/CORBIS; p. 138: AP/Wide World Photos; p. 142 (left): © Darren Staples/Reuters/CORBIS; p. 142 (right): McGraw-Hill Companies, Inc./Gary He, photographer; p. 144 (both): © Ryan McVay/Getty Images.